ORGANIZING THE TECHNICAL CONFERENCE

HERBERT S. KINDLER

Director, Technical and Education Services
Instrument Society of America

Illustrated by Joseph H. Calley

REINHOLD PUBLISHING CORPORATION, *New York*
CHAPMAN & HALL, Ltd., *London*

Library of Congress Catalog Card Number: 60-11875

Printed in the United States of America

It is the province of knowledge to speak
and it is the privilege of wisdom to listen

—OLIVER WENDELL HOLMES

*To Alex, David, and Peggy, who
wondered why Daddy spent so much time away
from home at technical conferences.*

Preface

This book is intended to help guide those who wish to plan or participate in a conference. Although technical, scientific, professional, and committee conferences, specifically, are discussed, the basic concepts presented will be of use to many other groups as well.

It is not the purpose of this book to show the reader how to organize a conference (or convention) where attendance ranges in the thousands, since such mammoth meetings are usually administered with paid staff assistance. Rather, discussion is focused on organizing smaller gatherings, considered by most technical leaders to be the more effective vehicle for person-to-person communication. Those concerned with large meetings, however, should also find many of the ideas helpful and thought-provoking.

All concepts are offered assuming that conference manpower consists of volunteers. If professional assistance is available, so much the better.

No single plan for organizing a conference exists. There are no pat rules. For example, advance registration may be desirable for a meeting of three hundred persons, undesirable for one of ten thousand. Evening hours may be satisfactory for a conference situated on a remote campus but unsuitable for one located in an urban center. To reduce the loss of precious manhours each year, when conference committees rehash the same old problems, a wide variety of conference methods are comprehensively discussed.

All conference techniques described herein have been tried successfully (under the conditions for which they were designed). Some, however, are more experimental than others. The "workshop" technique, for instance, intended for exchanging technical information, has been utilized by only a few groups. The distribution of "worksheets," or pre-conference orientation material, is not a widespread practice. Very few groups schedule their sessions during evening hours. Rarely are conference topics formally discussed over the dinnertable.

All conferences have one problem in common: they require action so far in advance of the actual meeting that the conference planners cannot afford to learn as they go along. They must be able to anticipate conference needs from the start. To help schedule and monitor conference activities, detailed timetables have been included in Chapters 3, 4, 5, and 6.

May I express gratitude to Mrs. Marilyn M. Rollins, Marvin D. Weiss, and my brother, Lawrence Kindler, for their helpful comments.

The problem of man attempting to communicate with man about everyday incidents is demanding; the problem of men attempting to communicate with experts in specialized fields is difficult; the problem of leaders attempting to communicate with leaders at the frontiers of knowledge presents a profound challenge. This book is concerned with that challenge.

HERBERT S. KINDLER

Pittsburgh, Pa.
April, 1960

Contents

ORGANIZING
THE
TECHNICAL
CONFERENCE

1   *Are Technical Conferences Really Necessary?*

A technical conference is a gathering of people who want to share, evaluate, and extend knowledge.

Knowledge, for conference purposes, cannot be defined in absolute terms. Because physical and human phenomena are dynamic with respect to time, the knowledge derived from these phenomena is also dynamic, and therefore its validity is transitory, or relative. To accept human concepts as absolute is to reject the search for new knowledge. For example, prior to World War II, textbooks stated unequivocally that aircraft could fly no faster than the speed of sound. If planners of technical conferences had accepted this limitation as absolute, aeronautic science would have been seriously impeded.

Technical conferences are vital because they provide a mechanism for giving maximum effectiveness to new knowledge; it becomes more meaningful when related, categorized, and integrated with knowledge which has already been assimilated. Knowledge is a mighty force when used to stimulate thought and action. The technical conference is a place where people having new knowledge can meet and interact. A successful conference channels knowledge to serve current and future needs.

The word "conference" is used throughout this book to embrace the following communication media:

Symposium—a presentation of prepared addresses by individuals or panels, followed by audience participation.

Workshop—directed group participation stimulated by brief, prepared addresses. A smaller round-table meeting may be termed a *seminar.*

Lecture—a tutorial presentation.

Clinic—a tutorial presentation with demonstration equipment available to participants.

Symposia, workshops, seminars, lectures, and clinics are the building blocks of technical conferences. Avenues of communication can develop when these elements are adapted to conference needs. A well-organized conference provides an opportunity for conferrers to exchange information, evaluate proposed ideas, cross-pollinate views, and extend knowledge.

Technical conferences, however, are expensive both to conduct and to attend. The prospective conference organizer must ask, "Is a technical conference really necessary?" He must evaluate the likelihood of reaching his desired goals through the conference technique. This evaluation may be based on an examination of the following objectives.

Exchanging Information. Mere exchange of information may not seem a sufficient conference objective, but even in highly specialized fields new knowledge is generated in such profusion that an exchange of really pertinent information is a refreshing experience. Medical scientists alone are confronted with over 100,000 new medical articles every year. Although the *Current List of Medical Literature* included over 100,000 articles in 1957, the compilers estimated that they listed less than half the total world medical literature for that year.[1] The technical conference cannot eliminate the need for literature surveys, but it can effectively focus attention on developing all relevant information in key areas.

The problem of exchanging information was dramatized at an international conference when a leading American scientist presented a highly specialized paper. A British Nobel prize winner remarked at the close, "I would like to congratulate you, Dr. Jones. I have been thinking along the same lines and you've beaten me to it. John Smith wrote a paper in the *Proceedings of the Royal Society* a few years ago in which he worked out the diffusion case corresponding to your air case. I wondered if you had compared coefficients. . . ." The American scientist replied, "I confess I did not know about that work. I wish I had because it would have saved me considerable time and effort."

This conversation between international leaders in a small segment of a specialized field illustrates that were it not for technical conferences, vital information might never reach the most interested individuals.

History is filled with examples of the need for finding improved means of exchanging information. Because of poor communication, Newton's calculus was independently conceived by Gottfried Leibnitz several years later. In fact, a list has been published of 148 major discoveries or inventions made independently by different persons.[2]

Although this book is primarily concerned with the exchange of technical, scientific, and professional knowledge, equally rewarding conference exchanges might be sparked by topics of general interest. What is behind consumer acceptance of small cars? What is the influence of Soviet industrialization on world trade? What is a community's educational responsibilities to its gifted children?

Evaluating Information. Technical conference discussion can yield incisive evaluations, but it should not be expected to produce clear-cut solutions.

Consider a conference exploring the problem of radioactive waste disposal. Assume conferrers agree that the problem is serious and urgent. Assume conferrers agree that within a decade radioactive waste will amount to millions of curies of twenty-year strontium-90. (Human tolerance for this radioelement has been set at one-millionth of a curie.) Suppose several proposals are presented at a technical conference for various means of safely disposing of radioactive waste before the waste disposes of humanity. One proposal suggests the construction of a space vehicle for rocketing the waste to another planet. Another urges that waste products be buried deep below the earth's crust. A third envisions a reprocessing facility for converting strontium-90 into a relatively safe element.

If technical conferrers, from 50 to 500 or so, were required to work out a final waste-disposal plan, they would more than likely create much heat, find little light, and arrive at no decision. Clearly, the technical conference is an appropriate forum for developing all facets of each proposal, leaving the ultimate decision to a smaller group. (The small committee conference is discussed in Chapter 8.) The technical conference, particularly the conference workshop, offers an unmatched opportunity for conferrers to evaluate the validity of proposals, weigh future possibilities, and suggest methods for testing likely solutions.

The technical conference has been used repeatedly as a sounding board for evaluating standards. Some organizations insist on discussing proposed standards with a representative group before issuance. However, responsibility for making the final decision lies not with the conference body but with the issuing organization.

Cross-pollinating Views. The trend of our sciences, professions, and technologies is toward specialization. The result is a complex of segmented knowledge which provides limitless opportunities for rewarding interchange. By placing one body of specialized knowledge in intimate contact with another, a rich and revitalized hybrid can be produced. Hundreds of hybrids have evolved out of the sciences and are still growing and hybridizing. In chemistry, for example, cross-pollination has produced agrochemistry, biochemistry, geochemistry, neurochemistry, physiochemistry, and radiochemistry. Science has recognized that no single view can do justice to all worthwhile potentialities.

The technical conference offers an ideal opportunity to weld segmented knowledge. Conference planners can often stimulate a new or slow-moving field by cross-programing it with a field that is more technologically advanced. The difference in technological development between two fields serves as a driving force toward creative results. For example, a more stimulating interchange might be expected from an electronics-medical program than from an electronics-aeronautical program. Electronics has already won wide acceptance in the aeronautical field and has even borne an offspring, "avionics." However, the advanced concepts and techniques of electronics have not yet been applied extensively enough to the field of medicine.

Opportunities for courtship between electronics and medicine might well be the theme of a conference panel or workshop entitled, "Potential Applications of Electronic Techniques in Medicine." Lively discussion could be encouraged by a few provocative topics such as the use of electronic controllers for dispensing anesthesia in direct response to a patient's physiological changes; the use of bedside electronic monitors for alerting hospital personnel when patients sink critically; the use of electronic computers for diagnosis.

Fruitful discussion often is sparked by cross-pollinating new developments in a more mechanized or automated field with old problems in a slower moving field. Within the framework of the electronics-medical conference, such a cross-pollinating approach might pit new transistor developments against old methods of diagnosis in internal medicine. Such a conference might stimulate an idea as dramatic as the "radio pill" developed by RCA and the Rockefeller Institute for Medical Research. The radio pill is a tiny FM radio transmitter enclosed in a capsule which can be swallowed exactly like an aspirin. As the pill travels through the gastrointestinal tract it transmits radio signals which provide diagnostic information previously unavailable to the physician.

Cross-pollinated bodies of knowledge may also bear fruit when two closely related fields are mated. One case history from the petroleum and automotive fields will illustrate the efficacy of this type of cross-pollination.

At the close of World War II, Gasoline Company X nationally advertised that their gasoline outclassed rival brands because it contained no tetraethyl lead. Not many months after this major advertising campaign, car manufacturers boosted engine compression ratios and concomitantly increased the demand for higher octane fuels. Company X was caught flat-footed. They simply could not produce the required octane ratings economically without adding tetraethyl lead to their gasoline. Clearly, a better marketing decision might have been made had adequate information been obtained at a technical conference between petroleum chemists and automotive engineers. (Ironically, several years after Company X was forced to add lead to their product, platinum catalytic reforming became commercially feasible as a means of producing high octane gasoline without additives.)

Extending Knowledge. One way to extend knowledge is to seek deficiencies in one area which are suspected of inhibiting progress in other areas. For example, conference programers might learn that a single technological bottleneck is impairing the reliability of missile components, limiting the peaceful use of atomic energy, and retarding development in jet engine design. Such a bottleneck was in fact the problem of accurate measurement of very high temperatures. Simply focusing attention on an unyielding problem may spotlight its general importance and trigger its ultimate solution.

Another way to extend knowledge is to select conference topics in fertile problem areas. For example, conferences might develop new knowledge by exploring the following:

No fewer than 1,000 American cities have been affected by water shortages. How can we extend our knowledge to ensure the economic growth of these communities?

Over ten billion checks were cashed in United States banks in 1958. How can we extend our knowledge to make the handling and accounting of checks more automatic?

About 750,000 chemical compounds are known, yet less than 5,000 commercial or medical uses have been found. How can we extend our knowledge to draw from the vast reservoir of available chemicals?

Unfortunately, new knowledge is difficult to anticipate because the results of basic research are so unpredictable. Fundamental research must be conducted without too much concern for the ultimate utilization of its discoveries. Conference planners have the opportunity to sift research findings to seek new applications. (Basic knowledge demanding appropriate application suggests a solution in search of a problem.)

The basic discovery of gas chromatography and its subsequent widespread application illustrates the catalytic influence of the technical conference.

Gas chromatography is the name given to a relatively simple procedure for separating multicomponent mixtures into fractions which can be quantitatively identified. It was discovered by a British biochemist, A. J. P. Martin, about 1932 while he was attempting to purify vitamin E.[3] The gas chromatography concept was first publicly stated in 1941—regrettably not at a technical conference—in a three-sentence paragraph of an article written by Drs. Martin and Synge for the *Biochemical Journal*. The concept was not utilized until eleven years later when, in 1952, Martin and James published a paper on the separation of fatty acids, in which they described a gas chromatography apparatus quite similar to currently marketed devices.

Since 1952, numerous technical conferences on chromatography have resulted in the extended application of gas chromatography instruments. Chromatography techniques are employed in many industries where applications range from analyzing food flavors to analyzing "aerosol bomb" propellants. But what if an alert program committee had revealed the potential of chromatography to the public in 1932? What if, instead of a two-decade incubation period, chromatography had enjoyed two decades of the spectacular growth experienced in the 1950's? The benefits to mankind would have been considerable. Surely it is a major challenge to any program committee to recognize potential areas for applying basic knowledge.

Tutorial Opportunities at Conferences

Generally, specialists attempt to stay abreast of new developments by reading professional, trade, and society publications. Yet specialist James Bright may not recognize where best to concentrate his limited time and energies. He may, however, learn of rewarding areas of study from those leading and experienced authorities who constitute a conference program committee. Such a committee can arrange educational clinics and lectures on topics deserving James Bright's penetrating analysis. For example, there is an increasing demand for engineers to learn how and where to use electronic computers. As part of an engineering conference, computer lectures explaining basic operations, coupled with computer clinics demonstrating potential applications on actual equipment, could render a worthwhile conference service.

A conference, however, does not offer the proper setting for exhaustive educational treatment of a topic. Rather, the technical conference should stimulate interest and point up areas for further study. Such study can then be pursued through appropriate texts, short intensive courses, or evening courses at regular educational institutions.

Was the Conference Really Necessary?

Following every conference, the organizers should evaluate this question in retrospect: was the conference really necessary? From the conferrer's viewpoint did the conference satisfy his objectives, his reasons for attending? When the last session ended had the conferrer exchanged significant information or substantially cross-pollinated his views? Had he evaluated ideas or had his own proposals been appraised? Had he gained new insights or really broadened his knowledge?

Conference success can be evaluated in terms of four basic interdependent elements. First and most basic, is the availability of worthwhile information, including both new and review types. Second, is effective presentation or transmission of conference information. The third element involves conferrer discussion, or feedback in the form of acceptance, rejection, modification, or amplification of presented information. The last element is the medium in which information is transmitted and controlled—the conference environment.

Persons interested in rating conferences numerically are referred to the Conference Success Rating Form in the Appendix. Here, the basic conference elements are expressed as equations which yield an over-all success rating.

Conference Responsibility

Planning and conducting, participating in, or assisting with arrangements for a conference program is a serious responsibility and a challenging opportunity. A technical conference cannot afford to be substandard. At best a substandard conference wastes manhours; even worse, a substandard meeting creates false impressions, half-truths, and distorted relationships.

Authority without responsibility can be dangerous. Any influential position imposes a responsibility to show discernment and objectivity, and to take effective action. The responsibility associated with conference participation or management too often is overlooked. Anyone who accepts an active conference role must prepare himself to exercise the inherent responsibility.

References

1. Brodman, E., and Taine, S. I., "Current Medical Literature: A Quantitative Survey of Articles and Journals," presented at the International Conference on Scientific Information, Washington, D.C., November, 1958.
2. Ogburn, W. F., and Thomas, D., "Are Inventions Inevitable?" *Political Science Quarterly*, **37**, 83 (1922).
3. Martin, A. J. P., "Past, Present, and Future of Gas Chromatography," presented at the Instrument Society of America's International Gas Chromatography Symposium, East Lansing, Michigan, August, 1957.

2 Initial Planning

"Let's hold a conference," suggests an engineer addressing a professional society committee; a professor chatting with colleagues in the faculty club; a foundation executive reporting to his board of trustees; or almost anyone speaking to almost any group with a common problem.

The response to the suggestion, "Let's hold a conference," is immediate, enthusiastic, and affirmative. The group agrees that a broad-scale technical conference is required to achieve their objectives, and that planning should start at once. A general conference chairman is needed—someone who is a good organizer and administrator; who knows how to draw effective people to the conference; who can motivate and work well with people, evaluate progress and results, obtain information, and communicate easily and clearly.

Let us suppose that the group asks *you* to be conference chairman. You have never before planned a conference. You are hesitant to accept the chairmanship—but you do, and you wonder where to start.

The right start is as essential to the success of a technical conference as is an opening gambit in a game of chess. Your most important first step is to organize a planning committee of members with diverse but related experience. If the conference topic were "Electronics in Medicine," for example, you might recruit physicians, scientists, educators, and engineers. For further diver-

13

sification you might seek men from engineering colleges, from hospital laboratories, from industry, from public health, and from private practice.

Sales-oriented personnel have a place on your conference planning committee only if they can subordinate commercial interests to conference objectives. Do not categorically overlook salesmen, however; their breadth of experience and drive can be a valuable asset to your committee.

While not absolutely necessary, it would be helpful to have two specialists on your planning team—one familiar with public relations, the other with technical publications.

The success of your conference depends on whom you select as committee chairmen and whom the chairmen select to serve on their committees. Who is a good "conference organization man"? He is not the "organization man" who William H. Whyte fears is being molded by our society. Mr. Whyte portrays a man who tends to lose identity, curiosity, and creativity. The man you want is more an idealist, iconoclast, and a self-starter.

Select your committeemen in terms of their self-motivation, creative and administrative skills, ability to arouse enthusiasm, knowledge of the field under study, freedom from commercial motives, and employers' backing.

Organize your first planning committee meeting without delay to demonstrate aggressive leadership and to reinforce committee enthusiasm before it subsides. If possible invite each prospective committee member to this meeting either in person or by telephone. Confirm in writing the acceptance of each member and notify the person in his organization who must approve his committee travel budget.

Your initial contact with prospective committeemen is a crucial step toward ultimate success. Discuss the significance of tentative conference scope and objectives. Show each candidate just how important the conference is to him, to his firm, and to the technically-oriented public.

How many planning meetings must you call before conference gears mesh? Don't try your fellow-volunteers' spirit of cooperativeness with a drawn-out series of meetings. Two initial planning meetings are usually adequate; sometimes one will suffice. A time-scheduled agenda will discourage loquacity. Distribute the agenda in advance, requesting that each participant come prepared to help resolve all items with "judicious dispatch."

During the first meeting, discussion may not always yield well-formulated conclusions. In such cases, assign to individuals or subcommittees the preparation of detailed proposals for action at the second session.

If the conference is to be sponsored by a parent organization, check the ground rules before your first meeting. Learn your area of responsibility and authority, and examine precedents and traditions. If the conference has a history, review recommendations of previous conference chairmen.

The following agenda may be used for your first committee meeting.

INITIAL CONFERENCE PLANNING COMMITTEE AGENDA

9:00 A.M. to 9:05 A.M.	Convene and introduce all committee members.
9:05 A.M. to 10:00 A.M.	Develop a statement of conference scope and objectives.
10:00 A.M. to 10:30 A.M.	Outline the program. (Serve coffee.)
10:30 A.M. to 11:00 A.M.	Determine conference location and dates, with alternatives.
11:00 A.M. to 11:30 A.M.	Establish a documentation plan.
11:30 A.M. to 1:00 P.M.	Luncheon (preferably in an adjoining room).
1:00 P.M. to 1:30 P.M.	Authorize a promotional plan.
1:30 P.M. to 2:45 P.M.	Approve an organization chart and set target dates for key activities.
2:45 P.M. to 4:00 P.M.	Draft a preliminary budget.
4:00 P.M. to 4:20 P.M.	Review assignments and summarize meeting accomplishments.
4:20 P.M. to 4:30 P.M.	Set a time and place for the next planning committee meeting and formally adjourn the present meeting.

To resolve all these agenda items quickly, yet thoughtfully, pre-meeting preparation by all committee members is essential.

The Planning Committee Meeting

In the role of general conference chairman and planning committee chairman, open the first meeting with informal introductions. Sketch the circumstances which led up to the meeting. Emphasize that the purpose of the gathering is to concur on objectives; to decide whether or not a technical conference can, in fact, achieve the desired objectives. If it can, proceed with the planning and organizing of such a conference. Usually those present will not only help plan the conference activities but also head the implementing committees shown in Figure 2.1.

Remember that you are asking your fellow volunteers for appreciable time and effort. Stimulate their initiative. During this meeting, learn the motivational influences to which they are individually most responsive. Beyond the desire to help achieve conference objectives, committee volunteers are encouraged by recognition through identification with an important and successful activity; recognition through advancement within the conference sponsoring organization; professional growth resulting from association with other volunteers; employer appreciation of their standing in the professional community as evidenced by conference leadership.

Conference Scope and Objectives

Decide for what type of audience the proposed technical conference should be designed, and how the group can derive maximum benefit. Limit conference scope to areas that have not received adequate study. Agree to a conference title which is both definitive and brief.

You may wish to organize a conference advisory board to assure that the proposed scope and objectives provide proper focus. Many leading scientists who are unwilling to serve actively, will be delighted to offer counsel in a high-level advisory capacity. An advisory board not only aids conference planning but also lends stature to the entire undertaking.

Take time to re-evaluate the probability of achieving conference objectives. If you find that significant information is inacces-
sible, that austerity is apt to prevent adequate attendance, or that
competitive conferences exist—consider canceling or postponing
your proposed meeting.

Although the initial planning session is timed to move at a
lively pace, a compromise in the schedule may be made regarding
discussion of conference scope and objectives; basic agreement
and sound conclusions are essential.

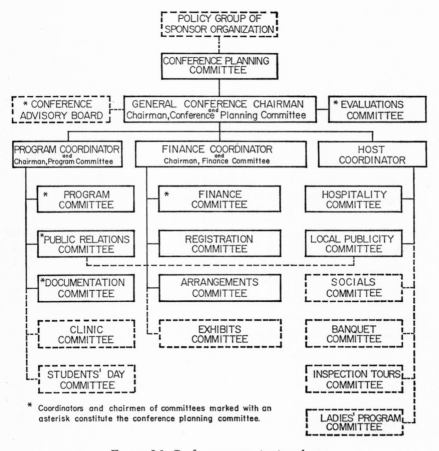

FIGURE 2.1. Conference organization chart.

The Program Plan

The program, as the heart of the conference, must be marshaled by an informed and resourceful program committee. To operate effectively, its members must acquire basic information from the conference planning committee. They must have a statement of established conference policies affecting the program as well as some indication of where the program committee itself is expected to formulate policy.

Conference Policies Affecting the Program. The following policies usually are set either by the conference planning committee or by the sponsoring organization.

Conference Level. The statement of conference scope and objectives should guide the committee in arranging a program on the desired level of communication.

Character of Papers Suitable for Presentation. Are papers acceptable which have been previously presented at other national or international conferences? Are papers acceptable which describe commercially marketed products?

Copyright Ownership and Future Publication Rights. If the organization copyrights all papers voluntarily contributed, does it also insist on copyrighting specifically invited papers? If an eminent physicist offers an important paper but is unwilling to surrender his copyright, does conference policy leave room for negotiation? How does an author obtain a release to publish his paper elsewhere after the conference? Answers to these questions should be based on the prime concern of the technical conference—extensive dissemination of information.

Complimentary Speaker Registrations, Mementos, Subsidized Expenses. Setting financial policies with regard to speakers involves maintaining a reasonable expense level (reflected in the registration fee) as well as good relations with the speakers. Some conference planners set unusually high fees for registrants with generous expense accounts to subsidize speakers who might otherwise be unable to attend.

Official Conference Language. For international conferences, the question of oral and written languages should be resolved.

Program Needs. Satisfying the following program needs is usually the responsibility of the program committee.

Facility Requirements. To expedite the selection of a conference site, the program committee should estimate such facility needs as number and capacity of meeting rooms, seating arrangements, and special utility requirements. Any needs which may affect conference site selection, such as a theater-in-the-round, should be emphasized.

Program Budget Draft. To help the finance committee arrive at a final budget, the program committee should estimate program expenses. Typical expenses include rental of visual and auditory aids, printing of question cards and conference notebooks, administrative costs, and fees for operating projectors and sound amplification systems. More unusual program expenses include closed-circuit television, facilities for simultaneous language translation, and projection equipment for 35-mm motion pictures.

Program Schedule. The program committee should not only schedule program sessions but also coordinate the scheduling of all conference activities to assure maximum continuity with minimum conflict.

Personnel. The program committee should be responsible for selecting qualified chairmen for all symposia sessions, workshops, clinics, and lectures. These chairmen, in turn, may be responsible for the selection of speakers, moderators, lecturers, and instructors.

Papers Review. Conference papers may be appraised for acceptance either by chairmen or by anonymous reviewers. Each paper should be evaluated against identical criteria codified in review manuals.

Supporting Activities

Appropriate supporting activities are those which will promote the over-all conference without too greatly diverting its energies from the central program. The planning committee should consider exhibits, a ladies' program, inspection tours, and social functions.

Exhibits. The question of whether or not to conduct an exhibit in conjunction with a technical conference has many implications. Professional societies themselves have widely divergent views on the subject. If the conference is conducted under the auspices of a professional society, you may be obliged to conform with its exhibit policy. Otherwise, your planning committee may puzzle the pros and cons itself.

Arguments which favor including exhibits are:

(1) The profits derived from selling exhibit space can reduce registration fees and can support conference activities.

(2) Exhibits are educational.

(3) Exhibits can be designed to dramatize the program theme.

(4) Exhibits complement conferences by demonstrating how conference theory is actually applied.

(5) The conference gathering presents a timely opportunity for conference attenders, responsible for equipment purchases, to see the range of commercially available equipment.

(6) Manufacturers learning of a conference related to their products often exhibit in "hospitality suites" at hotels near the conference site. However, suite exhibits are difficult to prohibit; they may remain open during conference hours; and may not emphasize the conference theme. A wise practice is to condone and control sponsored exhibits where rentals accrue to the conference organization, and hours of operation are regulated.

Arguments which favor excluding exhibits are:

(1) The conference organization is focused on creating an atmosphere free of distraction, conducive to an intimate interchange of ideas; great care is exercised to limit conference attendance, to balance conference representation, to distribute preconference orientation materials, to scientifically arrange conference seating—all to insure creative group participation. A commercial exhibit introduces a festive or "party" element which completely destroys the climate of serious communication so essential to conference needs.

(2) If the conference organization becomes dependent on exhibit income, exhibitor interests might compromise conference interests.

(3) Some outstanding speakers might shun conference invitations rather than link their names with what they may regard as a convenient excuse for, or an appendage to, a profitable exhibit.

Should the planning committee decide to conduct an exhibit, an exhibit committee would have to be organized. The planning committee would also be obliged to formulate exhibit policy concerning financial objectives, exhibit hours, relation of exhibit content to program content, space to be allocated to any one exhibitor, exhibit scope (that is, "table-top" displays as opposed to lavish "cubic-content" displays), and the proportion of complimentary "educational" exhibits to primarily commercial exhibits. One middle-of-the-road course is to furnish a manufacturers' literature area where vendors may place catalogs and leave business cards.

Ladies' Program. The primary purpose of a ladies' program is to improve conference attendance. If the location affords either pleasant recreation or good shopping, the wives may be quite willing to come along, and thereby influence the over-all turnout.

If a ladies' program is favored, a committee should be created to plan and conduct the activities of the program on a financially self-supporting basis.

Inspection Tours. Inspection tours may be encouraged if they are not concurrent with program sessions, if they relate to the program theme, and if they are located near the conference site. The tour committee's charter should suggest that tours be scheduled either preceding or following the technical program; that tours to plants, laboratories, institutes, computer centers, nuclear reactors be encouraged; that all tours be conducted and appropriate transportation arranged on a self-supporting basis.

Social Functions. When conferrers share each others' good fellowship, particularly at informal social functions, communication improves. The charter for committees arranging social functions need simply read: stimulate conviviality.

A policy statement is required concerning the financing of banquets, socials, receptions, and cocktail hours. Certain manufacturers may wish to finance conference socials for publicity purposes. Actually, such subsidization is often more of a bother than a benefit because fair play demands that all competitive manufacturers be invited to participate equally in the contribution.

Conference Location

Conference location should be proposed tentatively at the first planning committee meeting and settled definitely at the second. The following considerations should be weighed in narrowing your selection of a geographic site. Do geographic concentrations of people interested in your conference topic exist? If so, is one center of interest dominant? If no one place appears more logical than any other from the conference-interest viewpoint, then consider a centrally located recreational area that is readily accessible to airline, train, and highway.

The following factors may narrow your selection even further. Are facilities of special interest to conferrers available for inspection? Does the proposed location create problems of segregation? How do costs generally compare among proposed locations? If a professional society is sponsoring the conference, does that society have a local chapter in the proposed location? Local chapters will usually provide personnel to help with local duties because of their loyalty to the society, interest in the conference objectives, and desire to recruit new members into the chapter.

This is as far as you can go toward selecting a conference location at your initial planning meeting. Before the next gathering, an individual or subcommittee should investigate the site preferred and, if necessary, the alternative. The place chosen should conform to specifications of the program committee and to the following:

(1) A quiet atmosphere where conferrers will not be disturbed by non-conference activities—perhaps an off-season resort or university campus.

(2) Room accommodations within a reasonable price range, and the opportunity for single conferrers to "double up."

(3) All meeting rooms and smaller discussion rooms provided without cost and a complimentary bedroom suite made available to the general conference chairman or society president.

(4) Secretarial service and quick duplicating facilities.

(5) Dining facilities adequate for accommodating the entire conference group without creating annoying delays.

(6) Recreational facilities and lounges.

An interesting proposal regarding the selection of sites has been made by Dr. A. T. McPherson, Associate Director of the National Bureau of Standards. Dr. McPherson has suggested that a chain of specially constructed conference facilities be located across the country in recreational areas within reach of scientific centers, and that "Advanced scheduling, both as to date and probable number in attendance, would enable the conference facilities to be used fully and would thereby reduce the cost of operation below that of hotels or clubs." [2]

Conference Dates

Allow no less than a twelve-month preparation period between the first planning committee meeting and the start of the conference. Be sure that conferences do not conflict with other meetings or exhibits which may be of interest to your prospective attenders. Check previously scheduled dates with related trade or professional journals, or consult the publications listed at the end of this chapter. [3] Avoid scheduling conferences coincident with national holidays, religious holidays, or such sporting events as the World Series. Consider periods when schools are recessed if you want educator representation, if your conference location is a recreational center attractive to family vacations, or if you would like to use campus facilities.

Before setting definite conference dates, consult the local chamber of commerce or convention bureau for possible conflicts; local conventions or seasonal tourist influx can tax housing facilities. The chamber of commerce will also help you avoid special city and state holidays such as Bunker Hill Day in Boston, Discovery Day in North Dakota, or Andrew Jackson's Birthday in Tennessee.

Conferences of national scope should last two or more days to attract nation-wide attendance. A minimum duration of three days is recommended for international conferences. Travel generally favors conferences which either start on a Monday or end on a Friday.

Documentation

The planning committee must resolve the basic question of whether or not to document the conference and, if documentation is desired, to what extent and in what form?

Few persons will argue against compiling some form of written record of conference deliberations. The recurring point of contention is the extent to which they should be documented.

Individuals who oppose the one extreme, verbatim recording of everything, advance three principal arguments: life is too short to read all the drivel that appears on a verbatim transcription; complete recording inhibits free conferrer expression; access to complete recordings encourages prospective attenders to receive conference information at home without suffering the inconvenience of contributing personally at the meeting. Those opposed suggest that complete formal papers be published along with only the highlights of general discussion.

On the other hand, a dramatic case is presented by the "verbatimists." The verbatim camp digs through history books for its argumentative source material. It shows how well-documented conference workshops might have influenced medical history, for example, in the case of puerperal fever—the disease which once attacked women during childbirth with consistently fatal results. Understandably, few physicians had the courage to jeopardize their own practices by presenting formal conference papers on how their patients were dying of puerperal fever. Yet, had verbatim (anonymous) recordings been made of conference discussions, medical researchers might have deduced that the doctors themselves were carrying "death" to the delivery room; Lister's germ theory might have evolved much earlier.

The documentation committee's charter of responsibilities might be framed along the following lines:

(1) Publish transactions which include only material of enduring interest.

(2) Write special authoritative, introductory notes for the transactions.

(3) Exclude commercial advertising.

(4) Provide an author's guide for the preparation of transaction manuscripts and a reviewer's guide for their appraisal.

(5) Submit a statement of all documentation costs anticipated.

Promotion and Public Relations

Regardless of how progressive the conference program, appealing the supporting activities, or commodious the meeting site, a conference without conferrers is a dismal failure. Yet, George Freeman is typical of anti-promotional conference planners. Mr. Freeman told one planning committee, "We shouldn't have to go out and sell this conference. When I attended a recent farmers' meeting I noticed that they didn't talk about how to get the cattle to come to the rack. They talked about the best kinds of feed."

In rebuttal, Mr. Madison replied, "Mr. Freeman, conferrers are not cattle and cannot be led to a conference. They are busy men. We must reach them; we must compete for their valuable time; we must convince them that time spent at our conference is time well invested."

The planning committee need not concern itself with deciding exactly how the conference should be promoted. A competent public relations committee will "perk up" the conference story and disseminate it through appropriate channels, as described in Chapter 5.

The primary question for the planning committee is how much of the budget should go for conference promotion. A good approach is to ask the public relations committee for three estimates, one for an elaborate publicity campaign, one for a moderate campaign, and one for a "just-barely-enough" campaign. At the second planning committee meeting, while the over-all budget draft is being reviewed, an appropriate promotional expenditure can be decided on and can be specified in the public relations committee charter.

The Organization

The conference organization, like any other well-managed enterprise, must integrate individual activity with effective group action to achieve desired goals. The organization chart, Figure 2.1, illustrates one arrangement for joining separate units into an effective team. By staffing the planning committee with the three activities' coordinators and the key committee chairmen, a two-way communication channel is provided between conference planners and committee workers.

The operations plan can proceed on schedule only with good communication. Every volunteer must learn the significance of the conference objectives, the relation of his role to the over-all plan, and the job expected of him.

Suppose after the initial burst of interest a volunteer's enthusiasm wanes and his contribution to the conference effort seriously declines. You can either try to bolster his enthusiasm, or ask him to resign. Your schedule requires meeting target dates. Your organization must be capable of quickly detecting inadequate performance; every committee chairman and coordinator must have an understudy. You need feedback and backstops.

Target dates for the conference organization's key activities follow Chapters 3, 4, 5, and 6.

The Budget

Planning determines how objectives are to be achieved. Budgeting determines the economic feasibility of the plan. A budget, the focal point of all conference activities, predicts how financial resources will be used to implement conference objectives. Budget preparation must resolve any clash between the ideal conference plan as viewed philosophically and the attainable conference plan as viewed financially.

Because a budget should make the best over-all use of income, drafting the preliminary budget and approving the final budget are the planning committee's responsibility. Each committee whose activities involve expense should submit itemized costs to the finance committee for integration into a total budget.

The financial coordinator (treasurer) controls all expenses in accordance with the final approved budget. Financial control can be exercised by centralized handling of all contracts and monetary guarantees, by pre-approving all quotations over $50, and by disbursing all budget-sanctioned funds on receipt of appropriate invoices.

The one obstacle which must be faced realistically at the first planning committee meeting is that of initial financing. The two largest expenditures will be promotion and documentation. The major promotional expenses will be incurred before any conference registration income is received.

Most technical, scientific, and professional conferences are sponsored by organizations which underwrite initial expenses in the hope that the conference will be financially self-supporting. It is beyond the scope of this book to examine the various means for promoting initial capital. However, it is possible for the independent conference group to incorporate as a nonprofit organization and then solicit support from interested manufacturers or foundations.

Because conference costs vary so widely with time and place, the presentation of a sample budget might be very misleading. Instead, a conference check list follows to help guide budget preparation.

CONFERENCE BUDGET CHECK LIST

I. CONFERENCE EXPENSES

    A. TRANSACTIONS

        Quantity ————

        Printing process (Mimeograph, offset, letter-
          press) ————

        Estimated pages of text: —— × $——/page = $———

        Estimated pages of
          illustrations: —— × $——/page = ———

        (Page costs include all material and labor for
          printing and binding)

        Postage, envelopes, and labor for mailing
          transactions   ————

CONFERENCE BUDGET CHECK LIST—*Continued*

Clerical help .... _____

Complimentary copies for publicity, review,
   and committeemen: ____ × $____ =   _____

Copyright fee .... _____

B. CONFERENCE WORKSHEETS

Duplication and distribution $_____

C. PUBLICITY

Duplication and distribution of news releases $_____

Rental of mailing lists   _____

Poster preparation and distribution   _____

Printed "stuffers" for manufacturers to distribute   _____

Printed stationery "stickers"   _____

Paid advertisements   _____

Printing and distribution of _____ advance
   programs   _____

Printing _____ final program guides   _____

Clerical help   _____

Clipping Service   _____

Other: _____   _____

D. MEETING ROOMS

Rental charges or janitorial gratuities $_____

Insurance   _____

E. PROPERTIES

Projectors and screens $_____

Projection operators   _____

Sound equipment and operators   _____

Chalkboards, flannel boards, magnetic boards,
   flip pads   _____

Special utility installations   _____

Tape recording and transcribing   _____

Session question cards   _____

Other: _____   _____

F. REGISTRATION

Printed tickets, badges, forms $_____

Clerical help for advance registration   _____

Registration materials: receipts, indexes, badge
   holders, ribbons, cash boxes   _____

Registration typists and jumbo typewriters   _____

Preparation and duplication of daily lists of
    registrants   _____

Other: _____   _____

G. SPEAKERS

    Meals $_____

    Expenses   _____

    Hospitality   _____

    Mementos   _____

    Stenotyping   _____

H. ADMINISTRATIVE AND MISCELLANEOUS

    Printed stationery, questionnaires, postage,
      telephone, telegraph $_____

    Shipping costs and general supplies   _____

    Gratuities   _____

    Travel Expenses   _____

     $_____

I. CONTINGENCY

                 Conference Total........ $_____

II. CONFERENCE EXPENSES TICKETED SEPARATELY TO BE
    SELF-SUPPORTING

A. BANQUET

    Meals, gratuities, taxes $_____

    Professional speaker or entertainment   _____

    Special staging and lighting   _____

    Table decorations   _____

    Allowance for failing to meet guaranteed
      minimum   _____

    Printed banquet programs and tickets   _____

    Complimentary meals   _____

                 Banquet Total........ $_____

B. OTHER ACTIVITIES

    Inspection tours $_____

    Ladies' program   _____

    Socials   _____

    Honors and awards   _____

         Other Activities Total........ $_____

         Total of all Expenses......... $========

CONFERENCE BUDGET CHECK LIST—*Continued*

III. CONFERENCE INCOME

    A. REGISTRATION FEES AND TICKETS

        Conference fee: $____ × estimated attendance ____ $____
        Banquet ticket: $____ × estimated attendance ____ ____
        Tour ticket: $____ × estimated attendance ____ ____
        Ladies' Program
        Ticket: $____ × estimated attendance ____ ____

    B. OTHER INCOME

        Advertisements in the final program guide $____
        Donations   ____
        Other: _____   ____

                Total of all Income........ $====

There are additional questions to resolve before completing the budget check list. Shall reduced registration fees be offered to members of the sponsoring organization? Shall a registration fee discount be offered to advance registrants? Shall a special one-day auditor's fee be offered to encourage local attendance? Shall student discounts be granted?

Initial conference planning concludes with the resolution of these questions and the completion of the preliminary budget.

References

1. Whyte, William H., "The Organization Man," New York, Simon & Schuster, 1956.
2. McPherson, A. T., "A Proposed Standard for Facilities for Scientific Conferences," *The Magazine of Standards*, 202-204 (1958).
3. Various conference schedules appear in:
    a. "World List of Future International Meetings," Superintendent of Documents, United States Government Printing Office, Washington 25, D.C. (Part 1 lists forthcoming meetings devoted to science, technology, medicine, and agriculture. Part 2 records meetings in the social, cultural, humanistic, and commercial fields.)
    b. "Scientific Meetings, A List of Forthcoming Events," Special Libraries Association, 31 East 10 Street, New York 3, New York.
    c. "Engineering and Technical Conventions," 230 West 41 Street, New York 36, New York.
    d. "Convention and Trade Show Directory," 1212 Chestnut Street, Philadelphia 7, Pennsylvania.

e. "World Convention Dates," 24 Hempstead Avenue, Hempstead, New York.

f. Most professional and trade organizations publish annual schedules. Organization addresses may be found in the United States Department of Commerce "Directory of National Trade Associations," Superintendent of Documents, Washington, D.C.

3 *Program Development*

The telephone rings. A colleague asks you to serve as program chairman for a technical conference to be held in Chemburg. Your interest is aroused; you are sure of your employer's backing. You take the job. You attend all planning meetings and take an active part in framing the statement of conference objectives. You agree to staff a committee to implement these objectives.

How do you form a program committee? Start by making a tentative list of major topics. Find someone in each field with an outstanding record of achievement; invite him to develop a program session and serve on your committee. Be sure that your invitation conveys the importance of the Chemburg conference and the responsibilities of a program developer. If your invitation is rejected, ask for the name of another qualified candidate.

When your program committee is staffed, meet at a mutually convenient location. Plan on resolving all group questions. The only other committee meeting you will require is a last-minute coordination gathering at the conference site.

Include the following points on your first agenda:

(1) Select session topics; decide on the scope of individual presentations.

(2) Decide on the types of sessions (symposium, workshop, lecture, clinic).

(3) Schedule all sessions.

(4) Establish speaker responsibilities and privileges.

(5) Outline session chairman responsibilities.
(6) Suggest session vice-chairman responsibilities.
(7) Draft a timetable of program development activities.

Topics and Subtopics

As chairman, start your first committee meeting off in high gear by interpreting conference objectives, suggesting a preliminary program plan, and demonstrating how the proposed plan will achieve conference goals. This is a solid base on which to build a program structure.

For illustrative purposes assume that the Chemburg conference is on "Process Control in Chemical Plants." Its objectives are to explore the relationship between process control and process design, and unify the engineering approach to the problem of improving plant performance. The conference will try to bring together control engineers, process designers, and top management personnel from the chemical industry.

Your committee confirms the major topics suggested, and proposes three subtopics for each session. The program plan takes the following form.

Session 1—Introduction and Orientation
                Welcoming remarks
                Keynote address
    Subtopic a—Definition of process control
             b—History of automatic control in the chemical
                industry
             c—Concepts of process dynamics

Session 2—Present Status
    Subtopic a—How process control systems are currently
                engineered
             b—What the universities are doing
             c—Process control in Europe

Session 3—Economics and Engineering
　　Subtopic a—Shortcomings of existing plants
　　　　　　b—Economic considerations in plant moderniza-
　　　　　　　　tion
　　　　　　c—Optimum design for new plants

Session 4—Trends
　　Subtopic a—Direction of research and development
　　　　　　b—Computers for plant control
　　　　　　c—The plant of the future

Session 5—Problem Areas
　　Subtopic a—Reorganization needs imposed by "systems
　　　　　　　　engineering"
　　　　　　b—In-plant maintenance versus contract mainte-
　　　　　　　　nance
　　　　　　c—Educational requirements for process engineers

Types of Sessions

A lead-off session is normally presented symposium style with all conferrers attending. The keynote speaker may review the significance of conference objectives and suggest facets worthy of study. Other speakers may explore the implications of conference subjects; discuss and arbitrate conference semantics; set the stage for subsequent sessions. Leaders who have achieved national or international recognition often handle keynote speaking assignments with great ease and effectiveness.

The format of the session should not be decided on arbitrarily but, rather, related to content. If extensive research findings are to be presented or broad scholarly reviews programed, a symposium is indicated. If interdisciplinary concepts are to be unified, new theories evaluated, or information informally exchanged, a workshop is preferable. For purely educational purposes lectures or clinics are appropriate. Pure debate is not generally recommended because of its emphasis on competitive argument rather than constructive discussion. However, the debate technique can be extremely effective within a workshop for "provoking" group participation.

Referring to the hypothetical "Process Control in Chemical Plants Conference," assume that the program committee has settled on a symposium format for Introductory Session 1. Look back at the topics and subtopics for Sessions 2, 3, and 4, and see what type of meeting you would select for each one.

Session 2, "Present Status," would probably involve research and reviews, and therefore be most effective as a symposium.

A workshop format is logical for Session 3, "Economics and Engineering," to develop give-and-take audience discussion.

Session 4, "Trends," might warrant timely presentations. A timely paper may result in tentative conclusions based on incomplete evidence. While such a paper may not justify permanent recording, it may impel others to pursue the subject further. For example, when penicillin first became available to physicians, the results reported in medical papers at that time, though often inconclusive, were sometimes spectacular. Such reports hastened clinical studies of large groups under well-controlled conditions. Timely papers can be very effectively handled at a symposium using the panel presentation technique.

Session 5, "Problem Areas," suggests a workshop atmosphere where informal discussion can generate and probe new ideas.

Scheduling

The first conference session is crucial. Conferrers learn what is being offered in terms of their own needs. They learn what is in store for them and what is expected of them. Obviously, the entire group can benefit from this meeting. Don't make the mistake of scheduling it too early the first morning of the conference. Too often the opening session is set for 9:00 A.M. or earlier on a Monday. That the keynote speaker may miss his orientation breakfast is not too calamitous. What is more distressing is the slow procession of conferrers tiptoeing down the aisles during the keynote address.

Scheduling the second session poses an interesting question. Shall it be held in the afternoon or the evening? Evening sessions leave afternoons open for informal seminars, relaxation, and "idea incubation." However, evening sessions are recommended primarily for off-season resort or campus locations.

The next question is, shall program sessions follow successively, or shall some be held simultaneously? When two or more sessions are conducted at the same time, opportunity for cross-fertilization is lost, and "room hopping" may become a disruptive influence. On the other hand, workshop sessions are usually more effective when attendance is kept small; a number of workshops covering identical subjects may be run simultaneously, particularly if all conferrers gather at the close to compare notes.

The program committee is often consulted on the question of scheduling the conference banquet. If evening sessions are planned, the banquet may be changed to a luncheon, or eliminated in favor of a social or reception.

The final conference day should end early. To maintain good attendance after the last morning session is to battle with "human nature."

These scheduling suggestions can be translated into a time-table for the hypothetical conference on "Process Control in Chemical Plants."

Session 1
Introduction and Orientation Symposium
Monday: 10:30 A.M. to 1:00 P.M.

Seminars (both scheduled and spontaneous)
Monday: 2:30 P.M. to 5:00 P.M.

Session 2
Present Status Symposium
Monday: 7:00 P.M. to 9:30 P.M.

Session 3
Economics and Engineering Workshops (three concurrent sessions)
Tuesday: 10:30 A.M. to 1:00 P.M.

Banquet Luncheon
Tuesday: 1:15 P.M. to 2:30 P.M.

Seminars
Tuesday: 2:45 P.M. to 5:00 P.M.

Session 4
Trends Symposium (panel)
Tuesday: 7:00 P.M. to 9:30 P.M.

Session 5
Problem Areas Workshops (three concurrent sessions)
Wednesday: 9:30 A.M. to 12:00 P.M.

Speaker Responsibilities and Privileges

The conference organization has various responsibilities to its speakers. Conversely, each speaker assumes obligations when he agrees to participate. He should receive a comprehensive outline of his responsibilities and privileges along with his invitation to speak. However, before program committeemen can explicitly define speaker-organization relationships, they must resolve the following questions. (Answers to some of these questions will be found in the policy statements of the planning committee.)

Question. Shall speakers be paid or have any portion of their expenses reimbursed?

Discussion. With the exception of professional banquet speakers, men and women who address technical conferences are not usually reimbursed for speaking. The satisfaction and recognition derived from sharing their insights are compensation enough. Unfortunately, some of the best qualified speakers may be from government or academic institutions where conference participation is not financially supported. Also, some of the best informed speakers may live outside the country, and travel expense may be prohibitive. If the success of the program is jeopardized by a need for subsidies, the program committee should so advise the planning committee before any fees are set. A formula for registration fees may be designed to tax organizations which are most able to support the conference and its non-sponsored speakers.

An expedient way to increase international participation is to convince local industries to subsidize travel expenses in return for consulting services. Another way is to handle directly all transportation arrangements. On trans-Atlantic flights, for example, several airlines allow one free passage for every fifteen or so economy-class tickets purchased by a group. Such free transportation could be used to attract eminent speakers from abroad.

Question. May any individual voluntarily contribute his own conference paper? If so, do such individuals have privileges and obligations comparable to invited speakers?

Discussion. Broader and more interesting program coverage is possible when presentations of personally invited speakers are supplemented with papers contributed in response to general invitational announcements. A contributing speaker is usually required to submit a qualifying abstract for review. Abstracts are screened for pertinence, authority, timeliness, originality, and clarity. Invited speakers sometimes are granted one minor privilege not bestowed upon contributing speakers; they may be allotted extra platform time.

Question. What written material shall speakers prepare?

Discussion. The planning and documentation committees normally establish broad documentation policy. For the sake of discussion, assume that the following documentation policy—one of many workable possibilities—is established.

(1) All speakers shall prepare orientation material for registrants to encourage active participation at the conference. Workshop material, or "worksheets," may be little more than a collection of background sketches or a series of provocative questions. Symposium material may range from terse outlines to thoroughly referenced and illustrated manuscripts. Each author shall be free to decide what material will best "prime" registrants to contribute to his discussion. (2) Speakers shall be encouraged to submit

complete formal manuscripts to the transactions review board. While registrant orientation material is submitted in advance of the conference, formal manuscripts may be submitted at the meeting. Manuscripts are intended as permanent literature and must conform to specifications acceptable to abstracting and indexing services as well as libraries. The documentation committee shall codify all manuscript specifications in an "author's guide," to be sent to all speakers. The transactions review board shall accept for publication only those manuscripts which are mature contributions of enduring significance and which meet high standards of technical accuracy and clear expositional writing. (3) For ten days following the conference, registrants shall submit written discussions on any of the conference presentations to the transactions review board. Authors shall be encouraged to reply formally to all points of controversy.

Question. How are speakers expected to contribute to conference promotion?

Discussion. Promotional material must reach those people for whom the conference has been designed. Speakers may know and be asked to suggest persons who should attend the conference and institutions which should be represented. In addition, each speaker may be asked to draft a publicity synopsis of his talk, submit biographical notes and a glossy photograph, and suggest publications likely to be read by potential registrants. Some speakers may be requested to participate in one or more news conferences, or interviews on radio or television.

Speakers must be given answers to these additional questions.

(1) When a speaker plans his visual aids, what equipment may he expect the properties committee to furnish—2″ x 2″ slide projector, 3¼″ x 4″ slide projector, 16-mm sound motion-picture projector, overhead projector, opaque projector, micro-projector for microscope specimen slides, flip pad, magnetic board or "slapboard" for graphic displays? [1,2]

(2) May speakers use models and demonstrations?

(3) Will tape recording or stenotyping be used?

(4) What is the estimated attendance for each session?

(5) On what dates are publicity and program material due?

(6) Will authors receive complimentary copies of either their individual papers or of the bound transactions?

(7) Are authors required to surrender publication rights to the organization sponsoring the conference?

(8) Will speakers receive complimentary admission to all conference events?

(9) What kind of dress is required for the banquet?

(10) Will authors be expected to attend an orientation breakfast or social?

(11) Will any special arrangements be made to escort speakers from transportation terminals to the conference site?

(12) Where should registration, tickets, badges and ribbons be obtained?

(13) What is the exact time, date and place of the speaker's presentation?

The Session Chairman

Inviting Speakers. The basic responsibility of session chairmen is to achieve conference objectives by guiding program development and leading discussion.

Each chairman must invite all the speakers for his session. He should try to draw those best qualified without forcing half-hearted acceptances. While technical competence is essential, selection of speakers must be limited to those who can present their material effectively.

The following excerpts from letters of invitation to prospective speakers may prove useful.

". . . the objectives of the sponsoring organization, the American Science Society, are to advance the science of physics, encourage the personal and professional development of its members, and promote public awareness of the Society's services. . . ."

". . . the objective of the conference is to stimulate research in universities, foundations, and industrial and governmental laboratories. . . ."

". . . our session objectives are to report latest developments, analyze their significance, and generate ideas for future progress. Experts from the physical sciences and related fields will be encouraged to attend. . . ."

". . . material of an advertising nature is not acceptable. While trade names are normally omitted, the contributions or assistance of manufacturing companies may be included in an acknowledgment. . . ."

". . . despite the familiar expression, 'John Doe will read his paper, please *do not read* from your formal manuscript. What could be more unreasonable than to suggest to a conferrer that he spend three days listening to verbatim renditions of papers which he could study easily and with more selectivity at home? Instead, orient him. Stress the really significant points. Highlight the problems. Stimulate discussion. Speak conversationally. . . ."

". . . Reviewers will determine whether your paper is of lasting interest, and may comment upon technical accuracy and consistency. Editorial notes are offered in a sympathetic, constructive vein. You are always invited to justify your position. . . ."

". . . Prepare only essential visual aids. Allow three minutes to introduce, show, and explain each slide. Since you have been allotted twenty-five minutes for your presentation, plan on preparing no more than five slides. Keep slides simple and large enough to be read; meaning must be apparent. Consider the use of contrasting colors, shading, and cartoon art to dramatize your points. Number slides carefully and make a duplicate if you want to refer to the same illustration twice during your talk. . . ."

". . . If you believe certain points can best be developed through discussion rather than a formal talk, arrangements can be made to initiate audience participation. . . ."

". . . obtaining company and security clearance is the responsibility of each speaker. . . ."

". . . one of your associates should be familiar with your presentation so that he may substitute for you in an emergency. . . ."

". . . the program chairman has a special fund to assist prospective speakers who would otherwise not participate because of financial limitations. . . ."

". . . all conferrers, including speakers, are expected to live at the conference site to encourage casual as well as formal interchange. . . ."

Planning for Audience Participation. Most of us have endured lifeless meetings where the speaker delivers his formal talk and concludes by answering a few restrained questions from the audience. Since the collective audience possesses a pool of knowledge far greater than any single speaker, the success of a meeting would be assured if audience knowledge could be tapped. The following are tactics for drawing out audience knowledge.

(1) A month or so before the conference, when worksheets are distributed, ask pre-registrants to mail questions on any problems they wish discussed. This will provide session chairmen with insight into key areas of interest.

(2) Invite speakers to ask as well as answer questions. The impact of a direct question is sometimes all that is needed to stimulate audience participation.

(3) Hypothetical or disguised case histories can promote lively discussion. Often, at medical conferences for example, case histories are circularized beforehand to all pre-registrants so that each person may decide how he personally would tackle the problem. Then, at the conference, everyone has a chance to compare his conclusions with those of an authoritative panel—experts prepared to cope with a barrage of discerning questions.

The Fine Art of Chairmanship. Each session chairman must guide and coordinate all activities which bear directly on the success of his meeting. He must select speakers who are equipped and willing to present material pertinent to his session. He must arrange all the presentations in a logical sequence. He may call a special speaker-planning meeting to dovetail the talks for continuity, and avoid possible duplicate coverage.

Session chairmen should keep in close contact with speakers while they are preparing their talks—primarily to provide counsel, but also to monitor and expedite progress. Also, each chairman should learn enough about his speakers to introduce them properly at the conference.

A speakers' social or breakfast may provide a last-minute opportunity to check details and call the roll.

A real crisis arose at one conference of the Instrument Society of America when the keynote speaker did not appear at the breakfast. A call to the hotel—a special room had been reserved—revealed the disconcerting fact that he had not even checked in. While the vice-chairman was frantically preparing a substitute presentation, the speaker telephoned. Although his train had arrived the previous evening, his briefcase had been stolen en route. He had come into town late, without the notes for his talk, and without any idea of where he was supposed to stay. He was so befogged he couldn't even remember the time of the breakfast. Finally appearing with barely two minutes to spare, his address was one of the finest ever delivered to a technical society. The speaker was Norman Cousins, editor of *Saturday Review*.

The chairmen should *introduce* speakers who are not generally known to the audience, and *present* those who are well-known. Names should be checked for correct pronunciation. Brief orientation remarks should explain why the speakers were selected and how their talks will help develop program objectives. The chairman should conclude by turning to the speaker and repeating his name (into the microphone). This cue for the speaker to rise makes the transition from introduction to presentation smooth. The chairman should remain standing until the speaker has taken his place at the lectern.

Planning for any form of public speaking requires an appreciation of showmanship. Chairmen should arrange the seating on the speakers' platform so that attention is drawn to the individual at the lectern.

If a speaker appears to be running over-time, the chairman should warn him, by prearranged signal, to quickly conclude his formal commentary.

Formal presentations should be followed by general discussion. This offers the greatest single challenge to the chairman who must regulate discussion without showing partisanship, inject ideas to keep discussion alive, and summarize conclusions. He should repeat each question from the floor so that everyone can hear it, and so that the speaker may frame a reply. He should guard against any soliloquizing, filibustering, selling, promoting, or otherwise abusing the privilege of free expression. Such abuse was apparent during a session on education when pleas for donations interrupted the meeting. The chairman, quite correctly, discouraged the soliciting, though the cause was deserving, and brought the discussion back into focus.

Chairmanship includes such miscellaneous chores as calling regularly for breaks, reading announcements, relaying urgent telephone messages, correcting poor microphone technique, and guarding against any forms of disturbance. Should maintenance crew, for instance, start removing chairs from a backstage closet, it is the chairman's place to ask the workmen to leave. Also, it is the chairman who should summarize the accomplishments of the meeting, and thank both speakers and conferrers for their participation.

The Session Vice-Chairman

The vice-chairman has several important duties. First, he should understudy the role of chairman in order to take the reins if necessary and prepare for possible chairmanship at a subsequent conference. Secondly, he should assist with pre-conference planning and administration; that is, he should help develop the program, invite speakers, plan conferrer participation, monitor progress, and relay intercommittee communications. Thirdly, he should serve as "floor manager" during the conference while the chairman serves as "platform manager."

One of the most vexing problems that a volunteer conference organization has is maintaining effective lines of communication among its committees. An effective plan is to put each vice-chairman in charge of transmitting program information through a single program coordinator. (See Figure 2.1.)

Several committees require program information to function properly. The finance committee requires detailed estimates of all anticipated expenditures. The public relations committee must be continually informed of the program as it evolves. The arrangements committee needs a properties' check list for each meeting room. The documentation committee must examine all conference papers to see whether they meet transactions criteria.

The vice-chairman has the following "floor management" responsibilities:

(1) He must learn from the hotel or facilities management who to call for emergency service should such problems arise as power failure, poor heat regulation, or extraneous noises in the public address system. (At one conference, loudspeakers carried not only the lecturer's message but also a heated conversation between two waiters.)

(2) If he decides to trigger discussion by using question cards (distributed to each conferrer at the start of the session and collected after every paper), he should procure the cards from the program coordinator and arrange for their distribution and collection. Portable audience microphones may also be used effectively.

(3) He should make arrangements for a projection operator. In some locales, union professionals are required; in other places, volunteers may be "knighted" for the job. In either case, signals for changing slides should be pre-arranged; slides should be checked for proper position and sequence.

(4) He should arrange to admit only properly registered conferrers to the session.

(5) He should ask the hotel management that noisy repair work, electric floor waxing, or orchestra researsals not be scheduled directly above or below the meeting hall.

(6) He should test all properties to be certain that the equipment is ready for use.

(7) He should check all direction and door signs posted by the arrangements committee. Most hotels will list session titles, hours, and room assignments on their lobby directory. Some resort hotels will cooperate by announcing the start of each session over their public address system.

(8) He should help the evaluations committee arrange for the distribution of questionnaires.

(9) He should make a final tour of inspection before his session starts, to check the following items.

(a) *Projector.* Is the projected image sharply focused? Does it fill the screen? Is there a spare projector bulb on hand? Have the sequence and position of the slides been checked?

(A simple signal device between speaker and operator can be installed by wiring a push-button at the lectern to a hooded signal lamp at the projector.)

(b) *Room Lighting.* Have the switches that shut off overhead lights been located? (If feasible, install an overhead switch at the projector which maintains peripheral illumination to facilitate note-taking.) Have the shades been pre-adjusted?

(c) *Lectern.* Has the reading lamp shield been tilted so that there is no glare in the audience's eyes? (The lamp must stay on when room lights are dimmed.) Is there a pre-focused optical pointer on or near the lectern? (A glass and pitcher of water hidden from audience view on a lectern shelf may help the speaker through a coughing spasm without being a continuous source of distraction for thirsty conferrers.)

(d) *Microphones.* Are lectern, lapel, panel table, tape recorder, and audience microphones, if needed, properly located with adequate extension cords? Have amplifier controls been adjusted for good volume and tone?

(e) *Miscellaneous Supplies.* Are chalk, erasers, crayons, ice water, ash trays, question cards, note pads, and questionnaires handy?

(f) *Cloakroom.* Are the facilities for handling hats and coats sufficient?

(g) *Telephone.* Have room telephones, Muzak, and public address equipment been disconnected from all meeting rooms? Have other arrangements been made for urgent messages?

(h) *Ventilation.* Has the meeting room been "precooled"? (Body heat alone can raise the temperature of a well-filled room to a point of discomfort during the first hour.)

(i) *Other.* Probably more conference sessions are spoiled by speakers over-running their allotted time than by any other single factor. One vice-chairman used the following technique to discourage verbosity. He wired each lectern so that three minutes before a talk was scheduled to end, a warning light blinked. When a speaker's allotted time was over, a croaking horn sounded. Finally, if a speaker persisted three minutes over-time, he was suddenly engulfed in a dense cloud of smoke. (This technique is not generally recommended.)

TIMETABLE OF PROGRAM DEVELOPMENT ACTIVITIES

Negative (−) numerals indicate the number of months *before* the start of the conference. Positive (+) numerals indicate the number of months *after* the end of the conference.

MONTHS				
SCHEDULED	ACTUAL	ACTIVITY	PURPOSE	RESPONSIBILITY
−10½		Appoint all chairmen for the various program sessions. These chairmen constitute the program committee.	To have each chairman start planning his particular program.	Program coordinator
−9½		Appoint all program session vice-chairmen and aides; estimate room capacity needs.	To help plan each program and provide room reservation information.	Each session chairman
−9		Submit a detailed statement of all anticipated expenses to the finance coordinator.	To enable the finance committee to prepare the final conference budget.	Each session chairman and program coordinator
−7		Title each program session; decide the type of meeting; outline the scope of each presentation; invite speakers and transmit information to the public relations committee.	To crystallize the program and to provide news release material.	Each session chairman
−6½		Schedule all sessions; list the number and seating capacity of all required meeting rooms for the arrangements committee.	To arrange for meeting room needs.	Each session chairman and program coordinator
−5½		Obtain a 500-word qualifying abstract or preliminary manuscript from each contributing speaker-candidate; final conclusions of work under way	For chairman to review or, where in doubt, to transmit to	Each session chairman

MONTHS SCHEDULED	ACTUAL	ACTIVITY	PURPOSE	RESPONSIBILITY
		need not be included.	anonymous reviewers for acceptance, rejection, or modification.	
−5		Notify contributing speakers of the disposition of their proposed presentations.	To advise authors whether or not to proceed with formal manuscripts.	Each session chairman
−4½		Request each successful speaker to submit a 75-word presentation synopsis, his affiliation, title, biographical notes, and glossy portrait for the public relations committee.	For publicity use.	Each session chairman
−4½		Hold independent program planning meetings with panel and workshop leaders.	To develop unified program sessions.	Each panel and workshop chairman
−3		Obtain worksheet drafts or preprint manuscripts from all confirmed speakers.	For preliminary review and distribution.	Each session chairman; documentation committee
−3		Print question cards, notebooks, and other discussion material.	To increase the effectiveness of the meeting.	Program coordinator
−2		List all required properties for the arrangements committee.	To enable the arrangements committee to procure the necessary equipment.	Program committee
−1½		List all persons invited to each speakers' breakfast or social.	To permit the arrangements committee to reserve facilities.	Program coordinator

MONTHS SCHEDULED	ACTUAL	ACTIVITY	PURPOSE	RESPONSIBILITY
−1		Send final instructions about transportation, registration, and special activities to all speakers.	To remind and advise speakers of their responsibilities and privileges.	Program coordinator
−1		Ask pre-registrants to contribute questions for discussion.	To spark conferrer participation.	Program coordinator
−½		Enlist or hire projection, and sound system operators.	To operate equipment.	Each session chairman
0		Check to make certain that speakers have arrived, that facilities are ready, that signs are posted, and that all equipment is operable.	To insure a smooth-running session.	Each session chairman and vice-chairman
0		Conduct program sessions.	To achieve conference objectives.	Session chairman
+½		Submit complete reports of each program session to the transactions editor.	For incorporation into the transactions after appropriate review and editing.	Documentation committee
+½		Submit a final report to the general conference chairman on experiences, conclusions, and suggested improvements.	For compilation as a guide to future conference planners.	All committee members
+½		Provide the general conference chairman with names and addresses of all speakers and committeemen.	To send thank-you notes to all persons involved in the program.	Program coordinator

References

1. Casey, Robert S., "Oral Communication of Technical Information," p. 98, New York, Reinhold Publishing Corp., 1958.
2. Singer, T. E. R., editor, "Information & Communication Practice in Industry," W. I. Connelly, *Mechanical Aids to the Effective Presentation of Technical Papers,* p. 166, New York, Reinhold Publishing Corp., 1958.

4 Auxiliary, Supporting and Servicing Activities

The success of any conference depends on more than the excellence of its formal technical program. At least three additional activities deserve consideration.

First, should auxiliary programs such as tutorial lecture series, clinics or students' day events be scheduled? Secondly, should supporting activities such as banquets, socials, inspection tours, or ladies' programs be planned? Third, how should conference servicing activities such as registration, hospitality, and arrangements be implemented?

Auxiliary Program Activities

Lecture Series. Each conference represents an opportunity to harness some of the abundant technical talent available for tutorial service. Instruction by specialists may benefit those with different backgrounds. For example, an electrical engineer might lecture to biophysicists on computers; a communications engineer might lecture to neurologists on cybernetics; an instrumentation engineer might lecture to top-echelon management personnel on automation techniques. The tutorial lecture series is intended to satisfy a conferrer's desire for useful information related to his major field of interest.

One way to establish a worthwhile lecture series is to award lectureships as a tribute to outstanding achievement. The granting of lectureship honors and awards serves at least three purposes. Deserving individuals are recognized and often awarded monetary prizes; the problem of enlisting well-qualified lecturers is simplified; an avenue for additional conference publicity is opened.

Because the lecture series is an auxiliary activity, it should not conflict with regular program sessions. Three lectures followed by question-and-answer periods may comprise the series. If all three lecture topics are not of interest to the same audience, brief intermissions should be scheduled after each discussion period to permit some persons to leave and others to enter.

Clinics. Clinics—instructional classes which utilize equipment to teach current theory and practice (often entailing apparatus installation, operation, and maintenance)—are another tutorial service. While classes may be of interest to some conferrers, clinics often are designed for technicians. With the demand for highly trained experts continually increasing, the conference-generated clinic can offer a unique community service. The significance of the growing need for trained maintenance personnel is underlined by a predicted increase in maintenance cost to American industry of ten billion dollars between 1960 and 1965.[1]

Since the student body will be drawn primarily from local industry, the scope of clinic instruction should coincide with its interests. Ideally, clinic presentations should provide each student with a fresh approach and new understanding which he may profitably apply to his everyday job.

Oral instruction may be given in two parts. First, an instructor may present operational problems often encountered by technicians. Secondly, an equipment manufacturer or a conference speaker may describe principles of operation, give trouble-shooting hints, and explain preventive maintenance procedures and repair techniques. For example, a clinic class might cover repair of automatic control valves in an oil refinery. A petroleum engineer might explain how process acids corrode, viscous tars solidify and jam, and high fluid velocities erode valves. A control valve manufacturer might then explain how to replace corroded parts, how to dissolve solidified tars, and how to inhibit erosion. Formal instruction should be followed by discussion and "bench" work.

Clinics are best administered by a single committee rather than several other conference committees. The following are suggested clinic committee responsibilities.

(1) Obtain appropriate classrooms. Clinics scheduled for a week end either preceding or following regular conference sessions can usually be housed in local schoolrooms on a gratuitous basis. Obtain or furnish classrooms with blackboards, demonstration tables, projector stands, blackout shades, and 110 volt a-c electricity. Check nearby dining and parking facilities.

(2) Invite manufacturers to present topics which are related to the conference program and which will best serve the needs of local technicians. Assign specific topics, but encourage each instructor to develop his own detailed presentation. Advise companies against sales-oriented lectures.

(3) Furnish instructors from manufacturing firms with names of conferrers, employed by "user" firms, who may help present well-balanced curricula.

(4) Prepare an over-all schedule; assign specific but mutually agreeable class hours to each instructor. Schedule classes to provide sufficient time for companies to install their equipment and, subsequently, to remove it.

(5) Encourage all instructors to prepare multiple copies of their class notes on standard size, punched paper. Regular sales literature and catalogs are not usually acceptable. The clinic committee may collate, bind, and distribute class notes and notepaper to each registrant.

(6) Arrange for direction signs, classroom door signs, course schedules, and all registration material. Arrange for short-term insurance of equipment as protection against theft and vandalism. Send shipping and labeling instructions to each participating manufacturer.

(7) Concurrent classes will necessitate multiple sets of projection equipment. Consider resolving this problem by asking each manufacturer to furnish his own projector. Ask the companies to supply tools for the students, test equipment, and any special supplies such as bottled gas.

(8) Coordinate clinic publicity with the efforts of the local

publicity committee. Manufacturers may assist by distributing clinic programs in advance to local customers.

Students' Day. Conferrers can render a service to students of neighboring high schools and colleges by presenting a series of career guidance discussions, films, and demonstrations. The program should offer insight into vocational opportunities and requirements. From firsthand guidance, students can learn how to select a career and how to prepare for it. Who is better able to help students understand career demands and rewards than technical conference participants?

Conference Supporting Activities

Banquet. To arrange a conference banquet, the planner must imagine himself in the position of a conferrer. By the time a conferrer reaches the banquet hall will he be thoroughly saturated with technical talk and ready for a change of pace, or will he be fresh as ever and eager to continue?

Banquets feature after-dinner events ranging from "all-star revues" to philosophical addresses. Sometimes conferrer participation is stimulated by assigning problems to each table. Although professional leaders from all over the world may be seated around a banquet table, too often the typical banquet atmosphere is one of restrained "small talk." To trigger discussion, the following topics may be considered. What five research problems deserve top priority? How might educators better prepare graduates for industry? By what methods can new projects be "sold" to one's own management? What public relations programs are needed by the profession? How might the present conference be improved?

The task of planning and conducting a conference banquet involves the following responsibilities:

(1) The banquet committee should decide on the program. Menu selection can be assigned to one committeeman. (Consider religious preferences.) If the technical program and banquet are to be integrated, plans must be coordinated with the program committee. The arrangements committee should reserve hotel

facilities; the public relations committee should help design and distribute banquet publicity; the finance committee may be consulted about the price of banquet tickets.

(2) Ticket prices should be based on the following costs: food, gratuities, taxes, entertainment, special lighting, spotlight operators, floral decorations, publicity, meals for specially invited guests, and printing of tickets and programs.

(3) The banquet committee should plan the seating arrangement and provide for ushers. It is usually the general conference chairman's responsibility to decide who ought to sit at the head table and to arrange for place cards. General seating may be wholly reserved, partially reserved, or completely unrestricted. Non-reserved seating encourages "mixing."

(4) The banquet committee has primary responsibility for promoting ticket sales. Because the hotel must have a guarantee of the number of guests expected, refunds should be limited to tickets returned two days before the banquet.

Socials. There should be at least one social gathering during the conference. A banquet affords very limited opportunity for conferrers to mingle. A social hour immediately preceding the banquet is usually well attended and helps bring people with common interests together.

In planning and conducting a social, sponsors may be found among local manufacturers; however, much time need not be spent soliciting funds. Hotel arrangements can readily be made for "C.O.D. bars," where persons may individually pay for the drinks as they order. Soft drinks should be available. In some cases, hotels will agree to charge a little extra for each drink to finance platters of hors d'oeuvres. If the social is sponsored, arrange for appropriate credits to be given either on placards or in the banquet program.

Inspection Tours. Inspection tours may be a major attraction for some persons attending a particular conference. For example, a nuclear conference in remote Idaho Falls might draw people primarily to inspect the greatest concentration of nuclear reactors in the free world. Generally, however, inspection tours are frosting on the cake and should not compete with the regular technical program. Tours may be scheduled to follow the last technical session.

Planning and administering inspection tours involves the following responsibilities:

(1) The inspection tours committee should select the plants to be visited. Contact with each plant is normally made through its public relations director who may also help by furnishing publicity materials. The committee should determine the maximum size of the group, clearance requirements, tour starting time, tour duration, and the availability of luncheon facilities.

(2) Ticket costs should cover any round-trip transportation expenses between conference and plant sites. The inspection tour itself is usually complimentary.

(3) The tours committee should have tickets printed indicating tour date, and bus loading time and location. To assist persons using private transportation, tickets should also indicate the tour facility address and tour starting time.

(4) The tours committee should charter the required vehicles and promote ticket sales.

Ladies' Program. "I would have enjoyed the conference, George, but my wife kept nagging me about being bored."

A successful ladies' program does more than merely keep the women out of their husbands' hair. A well-planned ladies' program, with absorbing activities and an opportunity to extend acquaintanceships, can make the conference trip memorable.

The first requirement for an effective, smooth-running ladies' program is the appointment of a chairwoman capable of organizing a committee, investigating and selecting program activities, handling correspondence, maintaining a budget, and contributing almost all her time during the conference period.

The ladies' program committee should arrange the details of each activity, organize transportation facilities, prepare publicity material, arrange for program and ticket printing, conduct registration, help with receptions, and staff a hospitality suite.

The hospitality suite at the conference hotel is the ladies' registration, information, and social center. Here, women can meet informally for coffee, tea, bridge, and conversation. A "ladies only" lecture may be scheduled to give the women a clear picture of why the conference is important to their husbands.

If the conference site is a resort hotel, the social director may be of considerable assistance. He may help organize card parties, fashion shows, sightseeing tours, or "classes" on diverse subjects such as art, music, dancing, flower arranging, snapshot posing, or proper use of household appliances. If the conference is near a large city, additional activities may include theater and concert parties, boat rides, radio and television studio visits, museum trips, and shopping.

Usually, registration fees are set to defray all program costs which may include tickets, meals, gratuities, taxes, transportation, prizes, favors, and souvenirs. The chairwoman should be given funds in advance for necessary expenses and deposits. She should also be given a list of registrants, a few weeks before the conference so that she may send to each a letter of welcome outlining the proposed activities and suggesting wardrobe needs.

Conference Servicing Activities

Registration. The first physical contact between conference and conferrer occurs at the registration desk. Here, the conferrer will be either impressed by efficient planning or discouraged by a long, slow-moving line.

The concept of registration is simple: the registrant pays a fee and furnishes some information about himself in exchange for an admittance badge and some information about the conference. However, registration planning may be complex. What fee structure is equitable? Should the opportunity for advance registration by mail by offered? What information should conferrers be asked to provide?

The fee structure might differ for advance registrants and at-the-door registrants, members and non-members, self-supporting conferrers and subsidized conferrers. The following schedule of fees illustrates some of these considerations.

	FEE FOR MEMBERS	FEE FOR NON-MEMBERS
Conference registration (including transactions)	$12.00	$18.00
Conference registration (including transactions) for individuals from academic institutions and others required to use personal funds	6.00	9.00
Full-time students, excluding transactions	1.00	1.50
Single copies of bound transactions postage paid	5.00	7.50
Inspection tour transportation to research center	1.50	1.50
Single banquet ticket	6.00	6.00
Ladies' luncheon and fashion show	4.50	4.50
Ladies' theater matinee and transportation	6.00	6.00
Ladies' transportation to pottery factory	1.50	1.50

Advance registration reduces annoying delays at the conference. When a conferrer mails his fees and registration questionnaire before the meeting, he need merely pick up his badge and program guide upon arrival. Pre-registration also serves conference planners in that it indicates publicity effectiveness, helps determine required meeting room capacities, avoids extreme clerical demands, and permits advance mailing of conference worksheets and preprints.

Advance registration may be encouraged by the statement, "... reservations will be accepted and acknowledged in order of receipt. Total attendance will be limited depending on the facilities available. The registration committee may limit attendance from any one organization."

Pre-registration forms and fees returned to the registrar should be acknowledged; advance registrants should be informed when and where they may pick up admittance badges and tickets. Speakers and committeemen may receive special ribbons attached to their complimentary badges. Program guides and badges for advance registrants should be placed in envelopes, alphabetized, and indexed for rapid pick-up at the conference.

Thoughtfully conceived registration forms can elicit useful information if questions are reduced to a minimum. For example, suppose the question is asked, "Are you a member of the sponsoring organization?" The question, "Do you wish membership literature?" could be omitted were the decision made to mail membership information to all non-members. In addition to the schedule of fees, consider which of the following questions are pertinent:

Name:
Address:
Position:
List the products or services of the plant where you work:
What are your major technical interests?
Would you consider serving on a future conference planning committee?
Are you accompanied by your wife?
What publicity did you or your firm receive?
At what hotel are you staying?
What is the room number?

Admittance or identity badges should be printed well in advance of the meeting. Since conferrers usually wear badges throughout the entire meeting, a tasteful graphic design is a public relations asset (too often overlooked). Also, if a parent organization sponsors the conference, badges may be color-coded—differentiating members from non-members—to help membership promotion.

The registration area should be equipped with blank forms and pencils for at-the-door registrants; order forms for extra copies of conference transactions and other publications; conference preprints and samples of past publications; cash boxes with change and blank checks; receipt pads and rubber stamps with ink pads; admittance badges with plastic holders and ribbons; staplers; regular and jumbo typewriters; banquet tickets and inspection tour tickets; final program guides; ladies' program guides; colored felt-tipped markers and cardboard for improvising signs; banners of the sponsoring organization; supplies for return shipment of unused materials, including pre-addressed labels, scotch tape, wrapping paper, and twine.

Registration confusion at the conference can be minimized by posting prominent direction signs. Typical signs are:

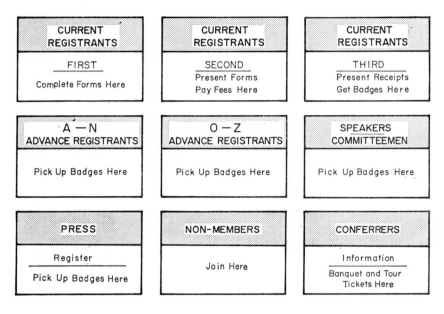

CURRENT REGISTRANTS	CURRENT REGISTRANTS	CURRENT REGISTRANTS
FIRST Complete Forms Here	SECOND Present Forms Pay Fees Here	THIRD Present Receipts Get Badges Here
A — N ADVANCE REGISTRANTS Pick Up Badges Here	O — Z ADVANCE REGISTRANTS Pick Up Badges Here	SPEAKERS COMMITTEEMEN Pick Up Badges Here
PRESS Register Pick Up Badges Here	NON-MEMBERS Join Here	CONFERRERS Information Banquet and Tour Tickets Here

It is often possible to hire registration clerks free of charge from the local Chamber of Commerce as well as to obtain special type-writers with jumbo characters. Clerks should be instructed to: (1) accept only completed registration forms; (2) type complete first names, not initials; (3) check registration form totals to verify cash; (4) arrange forms alphabetically if a daily list of registrants is to be prepared.

Information and Hospitality Center. The information and hospitality desk functions as a catch-all for many services.

(1) It is a clearing-house for messages.

(2) It is a sales agent for banquet and tour tickets.

(3) Membership promotion is sometimes delegated to information center personnel who are supplied with pamphlets and application blanks.

(4) Center personnel are prepared to answer questions related to program sessions, social events, committee meetings, recreational activities, facilities, and local points of interest.

(5) The center maintains a supply of local maps, Chamber of Commerce brochures and guides, and hotel floor plans.

Arrangements. The chairman of the arrangements committee must be a good "horse trader." He is responsible for obtaining the best meeting room facilities and properties for the least cost. He negotiates with the hotel sales manager cognizant that his delegates represent both a handsome income for the hotel and potential repeat business.

When giving business to a hotel, the chairman should require that public meeting rooms be complimentary; that one bedroom be provided without cost for every 100 bedrooms reserved by conferrers; and that public address equipment, lecterns, and blackboards be furnished free of cost. Occasionally, hotels will supply projection screens, but, as a rule, projectors must be rented or borrowed elsewhere. (Local committeemen can often borrow projectors from schools or research institutions.) These requests also are reasonable: Will the hotel hang a conference banner prominently in its lobby? Will it post a greeting to conferrers on the entrance marquee or lobby directory? Will it print a greeting on the daily menus?

More and more, hotels are maintaining their financial positions by courting conferences. Many have sales representatives on hand during formal conference activities to offer any assistance that may be required.

In return for hotel cooperation the arrangements committee should steer all social functions to the conference hotel and provide the manager ahead of time with a written statement of facility needs. A sketch of each meeting room (see Figure 4.1) will help hotel personnel arrange for facilities exactly as desired.

Hotels are willing to reserve blocks of bedrooms but require some means of identifying reservations. Positive identification is possible if conferrers address their reservations to the *Conference Reservation Manager,* for example, in care of the conference hotel; or if a conference-identified hotel-rate card is mailed along with each advance program.

Conference planners must understand hotel meal arrangements. Hotels require that a specific number of banquet meals be "guaranteed," usually twenty-four hours in advance. When an

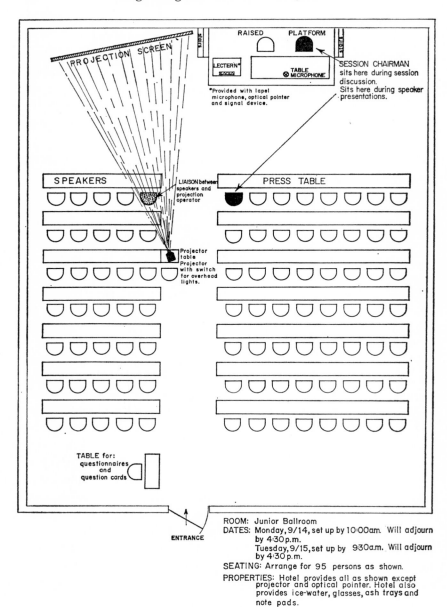

FIGURE 4.1. Meeting room layout.

organization guarantees 100 meals it is obliged to pay for them even if fewer dinners are served.

While banquet guarantees are a reasonable form of insurance for hotels, guarantees for small breakfasts are unnecessary. If, however, a breakfast guarantee is required, it is usually safe to give a low estimate; the hotel almost always will set extra places and scramble a few more eggs.

Cooperation between the hotel and the arrangements committee is essential for a smooth-running conference. Committeemen should be thoughtful about tipping for any special service they may receive. They should be prompt at mealtime. They should inform the hotel staff of any arrangements which might interfere with hotel routine. One maitre d'hotel tells the story of a well-intentioned, time-conscious banquet chairman who started dinner precisely on schedule, but neglected to inform the hotel staff of one detail. To the utter surprise and amazement of the staff, a boys' choir burst into song after every course. Imagine what effect such unexpected caroling had on the chef's broiling schedule, and on his explosive temperament.

TIMETABLE FOR AUXILIARY, SUPPORTING AND SERVICING ACTIVITIES *

Negative (−) numerals indicate the number of months before the start of the conference. Positive (+) numerals indicate the number of months after the end of the conference.

MONTHS SCHEDULED	ACTUAL	ACTIVITY	PURPOSE	RESPONSIBILITY
−11		Appoint chairmen for the lecture series, clinic, and students' day committees.	To implement auxiliary program activities.	Program coordinator
−11		Appoint chairmen for the hospitality, banquet, socials, inspection tours, and ladies' program committees.	To implement supporting conference activities.	Host coordinator

* (*Note:* Most conferences will not incorporate all the activities included in the following comprehensive timetable.)

MONTHS SCHEDULED	ACTUAL	ACTIVITY	PURPOSE	RESPONSIBILITY
−11		Appoint chairmen for the arrangements and registration committees.	To implement conference servicing activities.	Finance coordinator
−9		Submit detailed statements of all anticipated income and expense to the finance coordinator.	To enable the finance committee to prepare a final budget.	All chairmen
−9		Outline clinic topics, lecture series scope, students' day program, and general activities for the public relations committee.	To establish the auxiliary program and provide news release material.	Responsible chairmen
−8½		Outline all room requirements, facility needs, banquet seating, and the registration area layout for the arrangements committee.	To make hotel, rental, and loan arrangements.	Responsible chairmen
−7		Complete preliminary arrangements for plant tours, fashion shows, theater parties, bus transportation, menu selection, banquet toastmaster, and entertainment or featured speaker.	To assure success of these activities and to promote publicity.	Responsible chairmen
−6		Award national lectureships, confirm clinic instructors, and name students' day speakers.	To complete auxiliary program.	Responsible program chairmen
−5		Request each lecturer, instructor, and speaker to submit a 75-word presentation synopsis, his affiliation, title, biographical notes, and glossy portrait.	For publicity.	Responsible program chairmen
−5		Arrange for student attendance from local schools.	To assure a students' day audience.	Students' day chairman

MONTHS SCHEDULED	ACTUAL	ACTIVITY	PURPOSE	RESPONSIBILITY
—4½		Decide on final prices for all tickets, including transportation fees.	To settle the budget.	Finance committee coordinator
—4		Send a layout for the pre-registration form to the public relations committee.	To be included in the advance program.	Registration committee
—3		Print all tickets, badges, and forms; start acknowledging advance registration; start typing advance registrant badges.	To implement registration.	Registration committee
—2		Complete all advance details: print banquet programs; obtain hospitality maps, tour guides, and free tickets; get clinic insurance and arrange for protection of equipment; prepare registration and direction signs; complete final properties lists.	To coordinate completion of arrangements without a last-minute avalanche of unfinished business.	Responsible chairmen
—1		Send final instructions about oral presentation, transportation, registration, and special activities to all speakers, lecturers, and instructors.	To remind and advise speakers of their responsibilities and privileges.	Program coordinator
—1		Complete hotel arrangements for orientation meals; confirm final room arrangements for each program event.	To provide the hotel with required information.	Arrangements committee
—1		Send hospitality letters to all registrants for the ladies' program.	To extend a warm welcome.	Ladies' program committee
—1		Provide hospitality committee with complete data for the information center.	To anticipate likely questions.	Program, finance, and host coordinators

MONTHS SCHEDULED	ACTUAL	ACTIVITY	PURPOSE	RESPONSIBILITY
−1		Assemble note binders for distribution to clinic registrants.	To provide clinic students with permanent reference notes.	Clinic committee
−½		Complete final arrangements for registration material, typewriters, and clerks.	For registration.	Registration committee
−½		Complete final arrangements for program properties and projection operators.	To assure availability when needed.	Arrangements committee
0		Check that all properties are delivered and operable, and that all signs are posted.	To assure smooth-running activities.	Arrangements committee
0		Rehearse registration procedures with clerks; distribute written instructions, material and cash; check receipt stubs or forms to verify cash; distribute a daily list of conference registrants.	To meet conferrer needs.	Registration committee
0		Staff ladies' hospitality suite.	To make ladies comfortable; to provide an informal activity center.	Ladies' program committee
0		Arrange place cards at the head banquet table.	To assure proper seating.	General conference chairman
0		Conduct registration, lecture series, clinic, students' day program, mealtime activities, socials, tours, and ladies' programs.	To achieve conference objectives.	Responsible chairmen

MONTHS SCHEDULED	ACTUAL	ACTIVITY	PURPOSE	RESPONSIBILITY
+½		Mail refund checks.	To return advance registration fees to persons unable to attend.	Finance committee
+½		Submit a final report to the general conference chairman on experiences, conclusions, and suggested improvements.	To guide future conference planners.	All committee members
+½		Provide general conference chairman with names and addresses of all speakers, lecturers, instructors, and committeemen.	To help the general chairman express thanks to all persons involved in the conference.	All coordinators

Reference

1. "Automation Outlook," *Automation,* p. 4, February, 1959.

5 *Promotion and Public Relations*

P. R. Green was technical manager of Construction Consultants Corporation. Because of his reputation for clear thinking and lucid writing, he was appointed national public relations chairman for the Civil Engineering Society. When the Society decided to hold its national meeting at the University of Podunk, Mr. Green was called on to assemble a national public relations committee and appoint a local public relations committee chairman.

For the national committee, Mr. Green recruited an engineer engaged in interpreting research reports, a writer of civil engineering equipment catalogs, a purchasing agent familiar with printing specifications, and a draftsman with a flair for graphic design. An advertising executive agreed to serve as advisor.

P. R. Green proposed that the national committee try to attract qualified persons to the conference, and inform both the technical community and the lay public how conference issues might be important to them.

The aims of the local public relations committee were identical but on a smaller scale. In addition, the committee was expected to create in its locale a climate of understanding and an atmosphere of hospitality.

The national committee's first requirement was to gather information—the raw material of any public relations program. Conference coordinators were invited to the initial meeting to help answer the following questions:

What groups might benefit most from the conference?

How might these group be contacted?

How might the effectiveness of public relations techniques be measured?

A public relations committee, however, needs money as well as information. Mr. Green's committee designed a program based on funds authorized by the planning committee equal to one-third of the total conference budget.

Once the committee had evolved a program, determined how best to reach an interested audience, and requested an appropriation, the following media were considered: direct mail, press, radio, television, speeches, personal communications, proclamations, and student contests.

Direct Mail

Mr. Green believed that extensive distribution of detailed programs would be the most effective means of publicizing the conference. He found that he could rent mailing lists from professional and trade journals; however, mailing 40,000 advance program leaflets to attract 300 conferrers did not seem economical. Therefore, instead of distributing a multi-paged advance program, the committee decided to first circulate an announcement flyer.

Announcement Flyers. After checking postal permits and size requirements, the committee designed an announcement flyer for the following reasons:

(1) flyers would be substantially cheaper to print than the same number of detailed programs;

(2) because of the unusual format, graphic layout, and terse definitive "copy," flyers would capture the interest of qualified prospective conferrers;

(3) return cards requesting advance programs could be enclosed with the flyers;

(4) flyers could be stuffed with literature of manufacturers who might charge the conference organization just for extra handling costs.

Program. When Mr. Green's committee felt that the announcement flyers had aroused sufficient interest, an advance program follow-through closed the "sale." It offered prospective conferrers information enough to decide whether or not they should attend the conference.

P. R. Green and his committee, though tempted to distribute a mimeographed advance program, finally decided that letterpress printing would be more compact and would have greater "sales" appeal. The following points were considered:

(1) Statement of conference purpose. Title. Location. Dates.

(2) Who should attend. Why.

(3) Schedule of all conference programs, events, and activities.

(4) Name of each speaker with a synopsis of his presentation.

(5) Advantages of advance versus at-the-door registration. (Is registration limited? Are advance registrants mailed pre-prints? Do advance registrants receive an "early bird" fee discount? Are a few lucky pre-registrants awarded door prizes or fee rebates?)

(6) One or more tear-out pre-registration forms with the final date for advance registration.

(7) A routing form on the program cover for increased circulation.

(8) A form providing for direct confirmation of hotel reservations. Transportation instructions.

(9) A general information section explaining the operations of program sessions, clinics, students' day, inspection tours, social functions, conference publications, and the registration center.

The public relations committee also prepared a final program guide identical to the advance program except that pre-registration and reservation forms were omitted and the following items added: room numbers and exact hours of the meetings, the hotel floor plan, committee credits, taxi and airline telephone numbers, and blank note paper.

The committee realized, too late, that had it had just a little more information earlier the final program could have been eliminated; the registration and reservation forms could have been designed as center pull-out sheets, converting the advance program into a final program.

Other Direct Mail Pieces. The committee also mailed conference posters and gilt-edged complimentary invitations.

As part of promotion, conference posters were printed and sent to industrial firms, government and military agencies, laboratories, and colleges. The text, though similar to that of the flyer, was more graphically displayed. Interested individuals were requested to write for an advance program; a coded address enabled the committee to measure effectiveness of the posters.

To help create the desired atmosphere of understanding and hospitality, complimentary invitations (non-transferrable) were sent to select executives and civic leaders within a 100 mile radius of the conference site.

Press Relations

Conferences make news. Journals, newspapers, house organs, and wire services report news. It is up to the public relations committee to provide the press with accurate, newsworthy information. The easiest way to keep the press informed is to submit news releases.

The News Release. Editors receive many news releases during the course of a day, most of which are prepared by professional publicists. News releases compete for space. Those which conform to the following rules are most likely to be accepted:

(1) Use distinctive news release stationery to catch the editor's attention.

(2) Give the editor a release date, or state, "For Release on Receipt."

(3) Include the sender's name, address, and telephone number near the top of the page.

(4) Leave space for editors to insert their own headlines.

(5) Type double-spaced. Leave wide margins. Use only one side of the page.

(6) Start with a crisp, dynamic lead paragraph that cuts through the basic facts.

The following lead, drafted by a committee member, contains all the essentials.

"There will be another regular annual conference, the fourth, of the Civil Engineering Society on May 3-5 at the Union Building, University of Podunk. The keynote speaker will be Mr. Joseph R. Doakes of Los Angeles who will discuss the new federal highway program and related problems. Mr. Doakes is an engineer with the State Highway Department of California. Three hundred engineers from all parts of the country are expected to attend."

The committee reworked the first draft and not only reduced the text 10 per cent but also added pertinent information.

"Problems involving the new federal highway program, and affecting national economy and public safety, will be examined by California Highway Department engineer, Joseph R. Doakes, at the Civil Engineering Society's fourth annual conference, May 3-5, Union Building, University of Podunk. Experienced with Los Angeles' unique freeway problem, Mr. Doakes will stimulate discussion among the 300 engineers attending from all over the country."

Encouraged by the acceptance of its first release, the public relations committee sketched a complete news release program, outlining scope, scheduling release dates, and determining distribution. The consensus was that publicity for the Civil Engineering Conference at Podunk should focus on "economy and safety through better highway planning"; that all releases should stress some aspect of this theme. The committee used the following guide in distributing news releases:

MEETING CALENDAR ANNUALS

(*See Chapter 2, reference 3, for list of calendar publications.*)

(1) Distribute a calendar-format release. Give the name of the sponsoring organization; conference title, location, and dates; P. R. Green's name and address as source of additional information.

TECHNICAL AND PROFESSIONAL MAGAZINES AND NEWSPAPERS

(*See this chapter, reference 1, for list of principal directories.*)

(1) Distribute conference calendar releases for use in "coming events" pages of technical publications.

(2) As soon as all program topics are outlined, release a petition asking speakers to submit detailed abstracts for program committee acceptance.

(3) Arrange a series of releases to develop program highlights and report auxiliary activities. Time one release to announce the availability of advance programs on request.

(4) Prepare comprehensive releases for distribution during the conference. Use quotations to give a feeling of "live" reporting. (For example, "Today, at the Civil Engineering Society Conference, keynoter Joseph R. Doakes told a nationally representative group of engineers that a new road testing program in Los Angeles definitely reveals . . .")

(5) Prepare a roundup report after the conference to summarize achievements. Editors prefer that such releases be written in an "I was there" style. (For example, "The conference hall rippled with laughter when speaker C. M. Streat addressed the road engineers as 'my dear fellow highwaymen.'")

NEWSPAPERS

(*See this chapter, reference 1, for directory of U.S. newspapers.*)

(1) Feature local-interest items such as students' day, tours, clinics, and conference participation by local residents in releases to newspapers published in the conference area.

(2) Send releases to the hometown newspaper of each speaker; include biographical notes, a glossy portrait, and a synopsis in lay terms of his presentation.

(3) At the conference, give newspaper reporters a non-technical interpretive release explaining the significance of the meeting. (A sample paragraph for a local release might be, "Overflowing crowds heard University President William Johnson explain the critical need for strengthening civil engineering education. He set off a chain reaction of chuckles when he recalled how one newspaper, in a town where he had previously lectured, printed his message under the front page headline, 'UNIVERSITY PRESIDENT SHOWS NEED OF EDUCATION.'")

(4) Ask the ladies' program committee to write a few lines about those wives planning to participate. Distribute special releases to the social editors of hometown newspapers for use on the "women's page."

HOUSE ORGANS

(*See this chapter, reference 1, for directory of U.S. house organs.*)

(1) House organs (company publications for employees, customers, stockholders, and/or the public) often enjoy thorough cover-to-cover readership, and almost always use news featuring company employees. Accordingly, prepare individual releases on each speaker and committeeman for company publications.

COLLEGE AND ALUMNI PUBLICATIONS

(*See this chapter, reference 1, for directory of U.S. college publications.*)

(1) Most colleges publish periodicals in which space is devoted to class notes or alumni in the news. Send releases on speakers and committeemen to alumni publications.

MISCELLANEOUS PUBLICATIONS

(1) Slant news releases for Podunk's *Engineers' Club Quarterly*, the newsletters of local engineering and architectural society chapters; the Convention Bureau's *Meetings Bulletin;* the Chamber of Commerce publication, *Podunk Business Review.*

The Personal Visit. P. R. Green asked the local publicity committee to approach all local newspaper editors. He assigned various members of his national committee to contact a few key technical magazines and wire services to inspire confidence among editors and publicists, clarify written statements, establish background information, and kindle story ideas.

Mr. Green cautioned publicists against being overzealous in their efforts to sell news releases. He said, "Do not question an editor's prerogative to evaluate your news release according to his own criteria. He knows what is newsworthy. He is paid to decide if a release merits printing in full, in part, in revised form, or not at all. Bring your release to the editor's attention; give it proper focus, but never give it the 'hard sell.' "

The local publicity committee appointed Marguerite Pyle as its delegate. (In small communities, the newspaper staff may consist of one editor, or an editor and a reporter. In large cities, a managing editor supervises the collection and preparation of copy. Other editors who report to the managing editor, and with whom Marguerite might have contact, are the city editor, the business editor, and department editors. The city editor, responsible for local news, supervises a team of reporters, photographers, and writers. Department editors prepare general news stories, feature stories, editorials, and graphics.)

Marguerite Pyle called first on the managing editor of a morning paper and was cordially referred to the city editor. Her meeting was friendly but to-the-point; the city editor promised to assign a reporter to cover the conference. Marguerite, in turn, promised to meet the reporter and arrange several non-technical interviews.

As representative of the local public relations committee, Ernie Reston was asked to visit one of the major wire services. He learned that two leading services had bureaus in his city: Associated Press and United Press International. Science Service, a lesser known wire service that handles scientific information exclusively, has its national headquarters in Washington, D.C.[2]

Committeeman Reston was told that wire services carry only national or regional news. Items accepted in Reston's city would be relayed nationally by "trunk" wires and regionally by "district" wires to all newspaper subscribers of that particular service. He was also told that wire services are primarily concerned with timely, general-interest stories. One committee-prepared release which met wire service criteria started, " 'Future design of the family automobile may be radically affected by the results of current road tests at Autoville, Illinois,' said a prominent road engineer at the Civil Engineering Conference in Podunk today . . ."

Another committee member visited the managing editor of a leading civil engineering magazine in New York City. The editor was so enthusiastic about conference objectives and topics that he agreed to publish a conference issue one month before the meeting.

Bringing the Press to the Conference. A public relations committee should invite out-of-town press personnel only if it has newsworthy stories to offer which news releases alone could not handle effectively. Mr. Green's committee felt justified in inviting several key civil engineering editors. To make their trips profitable, the committee used the following plan.

(1) Only those editors were invited whose readers would be genuinely interested in conference topics.

(2) Invitations contained enough information for the editor himself to decide whether or not on-the-spot coverage was justified. Invitations were sent early and included a schedule of press activities; an advance conference program; an estimate of expenses; instructions regarding transportation facilities, hotel accommodations, and press registration procedures.

(3) When the editors arrived at their registration desk, they were each given a press kit containing a complimentary admittance badge and press ribbon, tickets, the final press activities schedule, the final conference program, news releases, captioned photographs, biographical sketches of colorful conference personalities, and background information about the sponsoring organization.

(4) A special press room, provided with typewriters, telephones, and an ever-present pot of steaming coffee, was staffed around the clock with a stenographer-typist and at least one committeeman.

(5) A press conference was called one hour before the first technical session. The major news break was the announcement that a one-lane highway test section was to be converted into a moving platform. A three-man panel covered different aspects of the conveyor project and answered questions from the press. After coffee and donuts were served, the unveiling of a scale model ended the meeting.

(6) A special tour of a nearby road testing installation was arranged to give editors and reporters background for the conference.

(7) Individual interviews were arranged to meet the particular interests of each editor; several feature stories blossomed as a result.

(8) A press row near the speaker's lectern was reserved at every session.

(9) The general chairman sent a thank-you note to the pub-lisher of each magazine represented at the conference.

Other Promotion Through Press Relations. News releases are distributed for publicity in the news, feature, or editorial pages of publications likely to reach prospective conferrers. Two other avenues for public relations are letters to the editor and book reviews. A letter to the editor is particularly effective for correcting misinformation or presenting the other side of a controversial editorial comment. Complimentary transactions should be sent to magazines that carry technical book reviews with the request that a clipping of the review be returned.

Radio and Television

Radio and television are primarily entertainment media. The successful radio or television publicist must tell his story with color, suspense, or humor; he must wrap educational content in a cloak of entertainment.

Betty Emerson, a member of the local publicity committee, was asked to visit radio and television stations in Podunk. During her visits, she met the station manager, responsible for administering the station; the program manager, responsible for over-all programing; the news director, responsible for news coverage and commentaries; and the special events director, responsible for extra-routine projects.

Miss Emerson had expected either haughty laughter or sneers when she told television executives that she had no appropriation. Instead, they listened earnestly to her programing ideas. She learned that in addition to commercially sponsored programs, stations "fill in" with sustaining programs. In fact, the U.S. Federal Communications Commission requires that stations allot time each week, without charge, to programs of public interest. Program managers must be constantly on the lookout for worthwhile material to satisfy FCC requirements.

The special events director was particularly intrigued by the prospect of a feature story on the new test road. The topic, he said, embodied many general-interest ingredients: timeliness, visual appeal, educational value, and entertainment potential. He, Miss Emerson, and a road engineer outlined the following television program based on the "news break."

The opening narrative, giving the history of the new road design, would explain how the conveyor operates, and how traffic problems might be overcome. (The narrator, an engineer, would have to speak with poised informality despite the clutter of studio lights, moving cameras, dollies, and booms.) The serious introductory exposition would be followed by a humorous skit—a family scene in the "car of tomorrow" as it is being pulled along on a superconveyor highway. The program would conclude on an educational note with a road construction film produced by the conference sponsoring organization.

Thus, using initiative and imagination, Betty Emerson succeeded in bringing one aspect of the conference to public attention.

Speeches

A community may be informed about a forthcoming conference through speeches to its local professional, business, and civic leaders. Luncheon or dinner talks can often be arranged with society chapters, civic groups, executives' and sales management clubs, and other local organizations such as the Kiwanis, Lions, and Rotary. These groups will be interested in learning why their city was selected as the conference site, why the conference topic is of value to them, and how they might lend a hand.

Speakers should be chosen for their ability to explain technical concepts in everyday terms without "talking down" to their audience. For example, with reference to the Podunk conference on highway design, one speaker at a Kiwanis meeting discussed the importance of road surface specifications. He translated surface roughness into dollars lost annually by every automobile owner as a result of wear and tear on tires.

Other Public Relations Techniques

Personal Communications. Probably nothing is quite as compelling as a personal letter or telephone call to stimulate conference attendance. Much of the appeal of a conference is its justification for old friends and colleagues to get together. The "reunion" provides an opportunity for off-the-cuff conversation, unguarded exchange of opinion, and comparison of ideas for solving specific problems. A campaign may be organized by encouraging all committeemen to mail at least three personal letters with advance programs to interested friends, and to extend at least one telephone invitation.

Proclamations. Additional publicity may be sought by asking the president, governor, or mayor to proclaim a special week in recognition of the conference topic.

Student Contests. The technical conference is an important event and could be the nucleus for worthwhile satellite activities. One such activity which the public relations committee might sponsor is a student contest. Certain technological fields such as electronics, astronautics, and nucleonics are "naturals" for capturing the interest of high school students. An essay contest could be the basis for awarding an all-expense-paid conference trip. Winning students might conduct televised interviews with conference principals. Student coverage of the conclave might eventually develop into colorful feature stories for both technical and general magazines.

Stickers. Bright, decorative, 2″ square stickers are eye-catching. Focus should be concentrated on the conference topic, dates, location, and where additional information may be obtained.

Stickers are a poor investment unless adequate means for distribution can be effected. The problem is getting people to use them in their everyday correspondence. One solution is to enlist the aid of committeemen and equipment manufacturers interested in publicizing the conference.

Paid Advertising. Economic conference promotion must be pinpointed to its target, not diffused. In view of typically modest conference budgets, paid advertising, whether press, radio, or television, is seldom feasible.

One effective technique is to ask interested manufacturers to cite the conference in their regular technical advertisements.

Photography. Photographs can enliven announcement flyers, programs, news releases, and, occasionally, television reporting. However, quality prints usually require professional photographers and may be a strain on the budget. Therefore, it may be advisable to obtain pre-conference photographs from the photo libraries of interested companies; ask press photographers who are covering the conference to donate extra prints; arrange for amateur photographers to attend the conference. Amateurs are often delighted to cover meetings in exchange for the cost of film, flash bulbs, and developing. They may be guided by the following rules.

(1) Capture action. A row of somber engineers or doctors staring into a camera is lethal.

(2) A crowded photograph is destined for the editor's trash can. Limit group pictures to four or five persons where individual names will be captioned.

(3) Identify all photographs by pasting captions either on the back or bottom of the print. Do not write on the back or use paper clips; indentations mar reproduction.

(4) Develop glossy black-and-white prints 6″ x 8″ or larger.

For the most economical distribution of photographs with news releases, include the following statement: "If you wish copies of the photographs captioned below, please wire collect and we will forward prints."

Newsworthy photographs may also be of interest to syndicates that distribute pictures by wire or mail to member newspapers and magazines.[3]

Successful Public Relations

The essence of successful public relations is having something important to say and saying it with sincerity and conviction to an interested audience. The first step is to collect facts; the second is to seek a common denominator and evolve a unifying theme.

The conference message can be directed to the right people only after a "market analysis" is completed. Who are the right people? Where are they to be found?

No amount of sincerity, introspection, or surveying will help, however, unless the public relations' voice speaks in a language that can be clearly understood. Consider how graphically Dr. T. H. Bullock has described the complex concept of neuron action in the human nervous system.

> "We now believe that the neuron is a functional unit somewhat in the same sense that a person is in society, in that it speaks with one voice at a time. . . . We now believe that the responses of many parts of the neuron to impinging excitation . . . help determine the firing of impulses . . . somewhat in the same manner as the impinging sights and sounds act upon the trigger finger of a man with a pistol." [4]

Public relations activities must be painstakingly planned not only to capture and hold interest but also to report facts with unvarying accuracy.

TIMETABLE OF PUBLIC RELATIONS ACTIVITIES

Negative (−) numerals indicate the number of months before the start of the conference. Positive (+) numerals indicate the number of months after the end of the conference.

MONTHS SCHEDULED	ACTUAL	PUBLIC RELATIONS COMMITTEE ACTIVITY	PURPOSE
−10½		Appoint public relations committeemen.	To prepare for distribution of conference information as it develops.
−10		Distribute the first news release featuring conference title, dates, and location.	For listing in the calendars of various publications.
−10		Establish public relations objectives.	To unify all public relations activities.
−9		Submit a detailed statement of all anticipated expenditures to the finance coordinator.	To enable the finance committee to prepare the final budget.
−8½		Distribute news releases outlining conference objectives and soliciting speakers.	To attract speaker-candidates for program committee considerations.
−7		Ask interested manufacturers to cite the conference in their regular technical advertisements.	To advertise without cost.
−6		Distribute announcement flyers and reply cards.	To obtain an advance program mailing list.
−5½ −3½ −1½		Issue a series of news releases featuring program highlights, key individuals, auxiliary activities, and conference goals.	To stimulate general awareness of conference objectives and promote attendance.
−5		Visit newspaper and magazine editors, and radio and television station executives.	To explore areas of mutual interest and to develop rapport.

MONTHS		PUBLIC RELATIONS	
SCHEDULED	ACTUAL	COMMITTEE ACTIVITY	PURPOSE
—4		Invite out-of-town editors of technical publications closely identified with the conference topic.	To encourage first-hand press coverage at the meeting.
—4		Distribute news releases about speakers and committeemen to appropriate hometown newspapers, house organs, and college periodicals.	To extend deserved recognition to individuals responsible for the success of the conference.
—4		Distribute stickers for regular business correspondence.	To stimulate interest.
—3		Mail advance programs; announce their availability via news releases.	To "sell" attendance to the most likely prospective conferrers.
—3		Distribute posters for bulletin board display.	To reach additional conferrer prospects.
—3		Institute a personal letter campaign.	To promote personal contact with professional associates.
—3		Mail gilt-edged complimentary invitations to local executives.	To create a local climate of understanding and atmosphere of hospitality.
—2		Complete arrangements for photographic coverage.	To help dramatize the roundup report and at-the-scene releases.
—1½		Instruct the arrangements committee about press seating for each program.	To enable the arrangements committee to provide the hotel with room layout information.
—1		Arrange for staffing the press room.	To provide expert help in arranging interviews and secretarial service.
—1		Send interested out-of-town editors final instructions regarding transportation, accommodations, and registration.	To demonstrate a concern for the guests' comfort.
—½		List press room properties for the arrangements committee, and press registra-	To insure smooth, cordial, effective press relations at the conference.

MONTHS		PUBLIC RELATIONS	
SCHEDULED	ACTUAL	COMMITTEE ACTIVITY	PURPOSE
		tion procedures for the registration committee; complete arrangements for the press conference, and for radio and television interviews.	
−½		Deliver speeches at local professional, business, and civic clubs.	To elicit local cooperation.
0		Telephone local newspapers to remind reporters of the news conference and special interviews.	To assure good press turnout.
0		Distribute press kits with news releases, photographs, and background information; conduct the press conference.	To encourage press coverage of conference activities.
+½		Release the "roundup report."	To facilitate coverage of the achievements of the meeting.
+½		Provide the general chairman with names and addresses of all publishers and editors whose publications were represented at the conference in addition to his own committeemen.	To enable him to express thanks.
+½		Submit a final report to the general chairman on experiences, conclusions, and suggested improvements; enclose a compilation of all mailing lists.	To guide future public relations committees.

References

1. The following directories, available at most public libraries, contain names and addresses useful in distributing conference information.

    DAILY NEWSPAPERS

    Editor and Publisher International Yearbook, Editor & Publisher Company, 1475 Broadway, New York 18, New York.

WEEKLY NEWSPAPERS

Directory of County and Suburban Home Town Newspapers, American Press Association, 225 West 39 Street, New York 18, New York.

COLLEGE PUBLICATIONS

College Newspaper Rate and Reference Guide, National Advertising Service, Inc., 420 Madison Avenue, New York 17, New York.
Education Directory, Part 3, Higher Education, U. S. Department of Health, Education and Welfare, Superintendent of Documents, U. S. Government Printing Office, Washington 25, D. C.

NEWSPAPERS AND MAGAZINES

Directory of Newspapers and Periodicals, N. W. Ayer and Sons, Inc., West Washington Square, Philadelphia 6, Pennsylvania.

MAGAZINES

Standard Rate and Data, Standard Rate and Services, Inc., 1740 Ridge Avenue, Evanston, Illinois.

HOUSE ORGANS

Printers' Ink Directory of House Organs, Printers' Ink Publishing Company, 205 East 42 Street, New York 17, New York.

RADIO AND TELEVISION

Radio and Television Directory, The National Research Bureau, Inc., 415 North Dearborn Street, Chicago 10, Illinois.

2. *Science Service,* 1719 N Street, N.W., Washington 6, D. C.
3. Wide World Photos, Inc., 50 Rockefeller Plaza, New York 20, New York. Acme Newspictures, Inc., 461 Eighth Avenue, New York 1, New York. International News Photos, 235 East 45 Street, New York 17, New York.
4. Bullock, T. H., "Neuron Doctrine and Electrophysiology," *Science,* **129,** 998 (1959).

6 *Documentation*

When a group of specialists come together and form an association, it is not long before they will decide to organize a technical conference. They may be content, temporarily, to record conference deliberations informally. Sooner or later, however, someone will propose that the association needs a documentation policy. The following case history illustrates how documentation policy is formulated and put into action.

John Gravure was asked to head a documentation committee. He started by listing questions for his committee to explore.

(1) What written materials help conferrers participate more actively at a conference?

(2) How can conference transactions best serve readers?

(3) What reviewing guides and procedures are needed?

(4) How shall conference publications be reproduced?

(5) What style and format specifications will govern conference authors?

(6) What editing requirements will have to be satisfied before manuscripts can be printed?

(7) How shall conference publications be distributed?

Preprints—Worksheets

John Gravure started his committee meeting off with a bang. "I guess we can agree that conferrers should receive preprints of each talk." The fuse was lit.

"Mr. Chairman!" voiced an earnest committeeman. "What purpose would preprints serve? How many advance registrants receiving a pile of preprints would ever find time to look at them? I suggest that we abandon the idea."

The program coordinator, invited to the meeting, defended preprints. "Anyone investing time and money to attend our conference deserves the opportunity to prepare himself for fruitful participation. While we must not permit reams of chitchat to be circulated, we are obliged to at least distribute terse, stimulating guidance material. Besides, from the program committee's viewpoint, preprints are the best guarantee that each speaker will be thoroughly prepared and will not improvise a hastily concocted talk."

Additional discussion resulted in the following conclusions regarding documentation.

(1) Instead of preprinting complete technical presentations, John Gravure's committee decided to substitute thought-provoking worksheets.

(2) Instead of imposing detailed format specifications, the committee decided to encourage authors to develop worksheets in any manner that would further their main purpose—to compel advance registrants to prepare for active conference participation. Author instructions were few and simple.

> "Be concise, clear, stimulating. You may state facts, pose questions, offer case histories. Try to construct your worksheet presentation on one or two typed pages. You may append tabulations, charts, statistics, and illustrations for reference and study."

(3) Instead of dissipating the budget by issuing two sets of publications, the committee decided to invest in quality printing for the transactions, and to produce the worksheets inexpensively. Authors were asked to mimeograph, hectograph, Multilith or otherwise provide adequate worksheets for each conferrer. If a speaker had no access to duplicating facilities, the committee assumed the burden. Worksheets, printed on standard size, pre-

punched papers, were collated into cardboard binders and mailed to each advance registrant.

Transactions Philosophy

After pondering, appraising, discussing, and restating the principles of a conference transactions philosophy, the documentation committee decided that transactions should be designed for cataloging in the technical literature of the world; transactions should include significant original information and comprehensive survey information; transactions should incorporate discussion and rebuttal of oral presentations; supplementary articles not presented orally but desirable as unifying elements should be specially solicited; manuscripts should be evaluated by discerning reviewers; transactions should be written, edited, and indexed to facilitate information retrieval; transactions should be well designed and typographically accurate; over-all responsibility should reside with an editor-in-chief.

Review of Technical Papers

Review is too often regarded as a malevolent device intended to obstruct the flow of manuscripts from author to printer. However, the necessity for critical appraisal becomes apparent after contemplating the amount of technical information printed annually. In 1958, some 55,000 journals were published containing significant articles about various branches of research and engineering in the physical and life sciences. More than 60,000 books were published in these fields, while approximately 100,000 research reports remained outside the normal channels of publication and cataloging.[1] To add indiscriminately to this ocean of literature not only would be a waste of effort, time, and money, but also might reflect discredit on the conference organization.

John Gravure's documentation committee agreed that a codified procedure for reviewing conference papers was required. A subcommittee, appointed to establish manuscript appraisal criteria, prepared the following form for manuscript evaluation.

Reviewer's Report Form

BASIC CONSIDERATIONS

(1) Is this manuscript intended as an original contribution? If so, is the information, in fact, original? Has it been previously published? Do you know of specific prior publications?

(2) Is this manuscript a review? If so, do you believe it is the most comprehensive one published to date on the subject? If not, can you cite prior publications which are more exhaustive?

(3) Is the information presented of permanent or transient value?

(4) Is this manuscript excessively promotional or commercial? If so, does it contain significant information despite its advertising nature? Can this information be reported inoffensively?

(5) Are major conclusions in this manuscript based on erroneous assumptions? What assumptions are incorrect, and why?

(6) Are major conclusions in this manuscript inadequately supported or illogically reached? Indicate poor substantiation or reasoning.

(7) Do you recommend publication of this manuscript in the conference transactions?

Complete the following section only if you recommend publication of this manuscript. The editors will correct grammar, style, and format. Reviewers should evaluate technical content and meaning.

TECHNICAL CONSIDERATIONS

(1) Is the title properly descriptive? If not, how would you change it?

(2) Is the scope accurately defined? If not, what is lacking?

(3) Is there a bridge between new information and already existing concepts? If not, what related materials should be included to help orient the reader?

(4) Are unusual terms defined? If not, which require definition?

(5) Is the text clearly written? If not, where is clarity lacking?

(6) Is the organization logical and easy to follow? If not, what changes would help?

(7) Are the references adequate? If not, why?

(8) Are the figures clear, helpful, and consistent with the text? If not, which should be eliminated or changed? Should any be added?

(9) Are any facts misstated? If so, how can they be corrected?

(10) Can the text be condensed, or irrelevant material deleted?

CONTRIBUTORS

Do you know anyone who might have pertinent data to contribute to this manuscript? If so, please give their names and addresses.

A technical paper may be suitable for publication if it meets at least one of the following three requirements stipulated by the Scientific Assembly of the American Medical Association. "Papers must (1) contain and establish positively new facts, modes of practice, or principles of real value; (2) embody the results of well advised, original researches; or (3) present so complete a review of the facts concerning any particular subject as to enable the reader to deduce therefrom legitimate, important conclusions."

What Every Documentation Committee Should Know About Printing

Selecting the appropriate printing process for any conference publication requires considerable study. The process must cost no more than has been allocated. It must be economic for the number of copies required; it must faithfully reproduce mathematical symbols, analog records, and microscopic slide photographs; it must give the desired professional appearance. Textual material or "line" reproductions may be printed by Multilith, photo-offset lithography, letterpress, or by mimeographing.* For photographic or "halftone" reproduction, Multilith (in conjunction with Xerography), photo-offset lithography, or letterpress may be used.† Basic principles of the various processes must be understood in order to determine the one method which will best satisfy all documentation criteria.

Mimeograph. The mimeograph process is used commercially to reproduce a limited number of copies from a stencil. Typing on a mimeograph stencil or drawing with a stylus displaces a coating impervious to ink, and exposes porous openings. The stencil is wrapped around an inked cylinder and then rolled over sheets of paper. The contact pressure forces ink from the cylinder through the porous openings in the stencil, transferring the typed text or line drawings onto the paper.

---

* The mimeograph process was originally marketed by A. B. Dick Company, Chicago, Illinois. Multilith was introduced by the Addressograph-Multigraph Corporation, Cleveland, Ohio.

† Xerography was originated and is being developed by the Haloid-Xerox Corporation, Rochester, New York.

Multilith. Multilith can duplicate a limited number of copies from a paper master comprised of typed text, pencil drawings, or Xerox facsimiles. (Xerography is a unique electrostatic printing process by which facsimiles of printed or photographed material can be transferred to Multilith masters.) The method of duplication from Multilith masters is identical to that of photographic-offset lithography.

Photographic-offset Lithography. Photographic-offset lithography, also known as "offset" or "photo-offset," can reproduce unlimited copies from metal plates; it is used extensively for commercial purposes. Material to be printed is pasted or carefully positioned on a paper "key" and then photographically reproduced on a metal plate. The photo-offset plate, like the Multilith paper master, is so treated that during the printing operation ink adheres only to the areas which are to be reproduced. Inked areas are rolled from the metal plate onto a rubber cylinder which offsets the image on paper.

Letterpress. Letterpress is a method of printing from raised surfaces and is used especially for books. The text is set in type and the illustrations are reproduced on metal plates by the process of photoengraving. Both the type and the cuts must be in relief. After the type and the engravings are positioned in form for printing, the raised surfaces are inked and pressed directly onto paper to transfer the image.

Printing Transactions

A study group, appointed to analyze the problem of how to print transactions, developed alternative proposals for the finance committee to view in light of the over-all conference budget.

Printing Proposal "A"—Moderate Cost Transactions. The object of this proposal was to outline a printing method which would render distinctive looking copy despite a limited budget. The group learned that for their purposes Multilith was the most economical process. They found that by using Varitype not only were there numerous type faces from which to choose, including mathematical symbols and Greek letters, but that right-hand margins could be aligned.*

The group proposed using Varitype with a modern type face having fourteen characters to the inch. Compared with standard typewriters which have twelve characters for elite or ten for pica type, the smaller but legible Varitype would reduce the number of pages and therefore the cost.

The group further recommended that drawings, charts, and photographs be transferred to Multilith paper masters by Xerography with captions set in Varitype. To help minimize expense, committeemen volunteered the use of their company's Multilith, Varitype, and Xerox equipment. Of course, all out-of-pocket expenditures for Multilith masters, paper, and direct labor would be charged against the conference budget.

Printing Proposal "B"—Deluxe Transactions. The object of this proposal was to outline a printing method which would reproduce an impressive transactions volume at a justifiable price.

The study group learned that the relatively high cost of letterpress engraving for the numerous illustrations favored photographic offset lithography; yet, the dignified appearance of letterpress typography was preferable. All illustrations could be separated from the text and grouped together. The text then could be printed by letterpress, the figures by photo-offset. Removing illustrations from their logical place in the text, however, might confuse the reader. Therefore, the group suggested maintaining text-illustration unity by combining letterpress with photo-offset.

The group recommended that all the copy for the text be done by letterpress but that only three or four impressions be printed; that the impressions be pasted on "keys"; that wherever possible the text be cut apart to provide space for the drawings, charts, and photographs. Then each key, complete with text and figures, could be transferred photographically to offset plates and printed.

Binding. The study group evaluated various types of bindings. Serious consideration was given to plastic and wire binding which permitted pages to open flat. However, such mechanical bindings

---

* Varitypers are made by Ralph C. Coxhead Corporation, Newark, N. J.

proved flimsier and more expensive than the side-stitched, wrap-around binding ultimately recommended for both proposals "A" and "B." In side stitching, wire staples are driven through the entire book; the backbone is glued thoroughly and secured by a flexible, wrap-around cardboard covering.

Paper Stock. The study group found that they had a wide variety of paper stock from which to choose. However, informed that special stock was required for each specific process, the committee completed their proposals by indicating the weight, tint, and texture suggested by the printers.

Preparation of the Manuscript

The following instructions should be sent to authors engaged in preparing conference reports.

(1) Write a comprehensive expository report covering the subject outlined by your session chairman. Upon receipt, we will have it reviewed for possible inclusion in the *Basic Research Transactions*. If your topic is only of passing interest and unsuited for the transactions, we will try, with your permission, to arrange for its publication in appropriate journals.

(2) Prepare a worksheet for advance registrants to encourage active conference participation. Use any style or format. Ask questions; invent problems; challenge conferrers. Include reference tables, charts, and any other data which conferrers might wish to study prior to formal publication. Make 300 duplicates for us to mail to pre-registrants. If you do not have ready access to duplication equipment, we will provide multiple copies for you.

(3) Deliver your report in such a way that audience participation is encouraged. To ensure complete freedom of expression, oral commentary will not be recorded. The press will be urged to report only discussion sanctioned by the speakers involved.

Our editing chores will be lightened if you observe the following rules when preparing your manuscript.

(1) Give your manuscript a definitive title—one that will be self-explanatory to future readers.

(2) Include your name and professional affiliation. If you are a member of the American Science Society, indicate your status.

(3) Organize your manuscript in the following manner (not necessarily including all items): statement of purpose, synopsis, conclusions and recommendations, body of report, appendix, nomenclature, references, bibliography, acknowledgments. Explain uncommon terms where they first appear in the text.

(4) Use superior numbers for references. Type the following statement at the bottom of the page where the first reference occurs. "Superior numbers refer to identically numbered references at the end of this paper."

(5) Write mathematical and Greek notations so that they can be recognized by our printer (who is neither a scientist nor Greek).

(6) Label all photographs, drawings, charts, and graphs. Identify each figure by number and a descriptive caption. For best reproduction, figures should be black and white (preferably glossy prints), and 6″ x 8″ or larger.

(7) In addition to your original manuscript, please prepare three carbon copies for our reviewers. Although your paper will be anonymously appraised, you may challenge any recommendations through your session chairman.

(8) Please give us the names of any individuals who may wish to supplement your paper.

(9) Double-space all typing. Number each page for the printer's convenience. Send your manuscript to your session chairman; he will relay it to the documentation committee for final editing and publication.

Editing Transactions

John Gravure appointed a university professor, Dr. Stettenheim, as transactions editor-in-chief. Dr. Stettenheim's first concern was to see that the conference program yielded an integrated transactions volume.

Conference objectives served as the foreword for the transactions. It read, ". . . to examine how basic research is supported in our country, to uncover obstacles impeding basic research, and to suggest means for strengthening the supports and overcoming the obstacles . . ."

Dr. Stettenheim proposed a comprehensive table of contents.

I. INTRODUCTION
   The importance of basic research to the future of mankind.

II. STRENGTHENING SUPPORTS AND OVERCOMING OBSTACLES
   What has basic research contributed to our economy?
   What is our economy contributing to basic research?
   What has basic research contributed to cultural progress?
   Where is basic research conducted in this country?
   What motivates the basic research scientist?
   Can basic research be a team endeavor?
   Is this country spending too much for applied versus basic research?
   How might students be further encouraged to pursue careers in basic research?
   How might industry, government, universities, professional societies, research institutes, and private philanthrophy be encouraged to support basic research?

III. CONCLUSIONS AND RECOMMENDATIONS
   Basic research—challenge and opportunity.

The program committee adopted the above preliminary outline and ultimately acquired manuscripts which became the foundation for a cohesive transactions volume. Where important topics were not adequately covered orally, Dr. Stettenheim requested supplementary articles. Manuscripts, supplementary articles, and written discussion were all carefully reviewed.

In close communication with authors, reviewers, and contributors, the entire volume was edited for accuracy, consistency, clarity, conciseness, organization, impartiality, and grammar. The editors did not alter style unless the intended meaning was obscure, and they cleared all editorial changes which might affect even a nuance of meaning.

Dr. Stettenheim emphasized the importance of all reference material being meticulously indexed. Accordingly, when page proofs of the transactions were available, index entries were circled and later copied on three-by-five inch cards. Separate cards were used for every entry and sub-entry, and later were alphabetized.[2]

A bibliography task force was organized to compile annotated references which made up the appendix.

Dr. Stettenheim supervised general format and proofreading of the manuscripts.

Distribution of Transactions

Preparing conference transactions is, in a sense, anticlimactic. Work still remains after the last echoes of the conference gathering have faded away. Even after a dedicated documentation committee has put forth a final spurt of energy to publish the transactions, its chores are not over. Transactions still must be distributed. In fact, the very reasons for holding the conference may be largely defeated if oral reports, observations, conclusions, and recommendations do not go beyond the conclave.

Transactions must reach key people if duplicated work is to be avoided. Conference information can be utilized extensively only if transactions are referenced in index and abstract compilations; if transactions are always available at a well-publicized source; if transactions are directed to technical library shelves.

The first step toward assuring adequate distribution of transactions is to apply for a Library of Congress catalog card number, before publication, from the Card Division of the Library, Washington 25, D.C. If the documentation committee should overlook this, the Library will assign a card number when the copyright application is filed. To appy for a copyright it is necessary to send a nominal fee, a completed and notarized form, and two copies of the transactions to the Register of Copyrights. A notice of copyright usually appears either on the title page or the page following in this form: Copyright; year of publication; name of organization claiming the copyright. The Library of Congress catalog number should be printed below the copyright notice.

The Library of Congress will categorize, catalog, and publicize the transactions, issuing cards to some 10,000 subscribers. John Sherrod,[3] Chief of the Library's Science and Technology Division, illustrates how the Library tries to codify references into bibliographies with the example, "Snow Ice and Permafrost Bibliography." Since 1951, "... more than 16,000 abstracts have been published in 12 volumes ... covering material published since the 18th century in 24 different languages." Obviously, when conference transactions are cross-referenced in Library of Congress bibliographies, they are firmly interwoven into the fabric of world literature.

To ensure adequate distribution of transactions the following program is recommended.

(1) As soon as the first volumes are printed, distribute complimentary copies to interested editors for review in their journals.

(2) Encourage editors of key journals to publish orally presented papers omitted from the transactions. Permit reprinting of transaction papers, abstracts, or excerpts with appropriate credits.

(3) Send transactions to each entitled conferrer, author, and committeeman. Ask each recipient to complete a postage-paid return card listing his firm's librarian and others who might wish transactions information.

(4) Distribute press releases announcing the availability of transactions to all technical publications even marginally interested in the conference topic.

(5) Send transactions information and order forms to non-registrants on conference publicity lists.

(6) To accommodate future sales, supply the conference sponsor with a transactions inventory. If the conference has no permanent sponsor, negotiate with an agency—a professional society, university, or research institute—to sell transactions and provide photostat service.

(7) Announce the availability of transactions to abstracting and indexing services. *Information Systems in Documentation* [4] list 312 index and abstract publications.

(8) Offer libraries a special discount. Library addresses are listed, and their special interests identified, in *American Library Directory,* published by R. R. Bowker Co., 62 West 45 Street, New York 36; and in *Special Libraries Association Directory,* 31 East 10th Street, New York 3. The American Library Association, 50 East Huron Street, Chicago 11, will rent mailing lists covering specialized libraries associated with research and agriculture, medicine, business, and law.

Directing Transactions to Libraries. Libraries are the hunting grounds for those in search of information. Miss Jones is librarian of an industrial reference library. She initiates the purchase of new books and periodicals. (Her firm's research director approves all orders for new library acquisitions.)

There are several ways in which Miss Jones is made aware of the availability of new transactions. She scans the list of new publications in *Publishers' Weekly.* She gives subscription solicitations from conference organizations her earnest consideration. Even more compelling are recurring requests for transactions from regular library patrons. After repeatedly borrowing transactions on inter-library loans and paying for photostat copies, Miss Jones may enter a transactions subscription. When she acquires a number of transactions in a series and finds them to be in persistent demand, she may also order back volumes.

TIMETABLE OF DOCUMENTATION ACTIVITIES

Negative (−) numerals indicate the number of months before the start of the conference. Positive (+) numerals indicate the numer of months after the end of the conference.

MONTHS		DOCUMENTATION	
SCHEDULED	ACTUAL	COMMITTEE ACTIVITY	PURPOSE
−10½		Appoint documentation committeemen including a transactions editor-in-chief.	To translate conference objectives into a unified publications program.
−10		Establish a documentation plan—materials to be prepared and duplicated; how; by whom; when.	To record worthwhile conference information in the most usable form; to delegate responsibilities; to establish budget needs.
−9		Submit anticipated expenditures to the finance coordinator.	To enable the finance committee to prepare an overall conference budget.
−9		Specify printing and binding processes for conference publications.	To produce easily readable, durably assembled, and financially feasible conference literature.
−5		Send instructions for the preparation and submission of pre-conference material to authors.	To help authors develop material which will stimulate conferrer interest.

TIMETABLE OF DOCUMENTATION ACTIVITIES—*Continued*

MONTHS SCHEDULED	ACTUAL	DOCUMENTATION COMMITTEE ACTIVITY	PURPOSE
−5		Inform prospective authors of transactions philosophy, format requirements, schedules, and procedures for review, written discussion, and rebuttal.	To help authors prepare acceptable manuscripts which will require little editing.
−4		Apply for a library of Congress catalog card number.	To obtain a catalog number early enough for printing in the transactions.
−3		Codify reviewing criteria and procedures.	To develop reviewers' guides for promoting thorough, constructive, and uniform appraisals.
−1		Mail pre-conference worksheets to advance registrants; include reference information.	To help broaden and enliven conference participation; to provide reference data months before transactions are published.
0		Deliver all manuscripts to the editor.	To enable the editor, together with authors, reviewers, and contributors, to publish accurate, lucid, well-organized transactions.
+½		Appoint individuals to record important aspects of discussion for reports to the transactions editor.	To provide the editor with material which might improve continuity of the transactions.
+½		Invite written discussion.	For inclusion in the transactions after appropriate review; for relaying to authors for rebuttal.
+1		Authors may submit rebuttal to written discussion.	To make certain that authors will have "the last word."
+1		Encourage journal editors to publish manuscripts considered inappropriate for the transactions.	To promptly release information which may be timely rather than enduring.
+2½		Complete indexing when page proofs are available.	To make transactions information readily accessible.

MONTHS SCHEDULED	ACTUAL	DOCUMENTATION COMMITTEE ACTIVITY	PURPOSE
+3½		Distribute transactions to registrants, authors, committeemen, and subscribers.	To provide workers in the conference field with a permanent reference.
+3½		Distribute transactions to interested abstracting services and book reviewers; distribute announcements and news releases to journals and potential subscribers including libraries.	To make known the availability of transactions.
+4		Authorize an established agency to sell transactions.	To accommodate future purchase orders.
+4		Apply for copyright.	To make certain that transactions will be cataloged by and placed in the Library of Congress, and will be listed in the *Cumulative Book Index,* published by H. W. Wilson Company.
+4		Provide the general chairman with names and addresses of all documentation committeemen.	To enable him to express thanks.
+4		Submit a final report to the general conference chairman on experiences, conclusions, and suggested improvements.	To guide future documentation committees.

References

1. Killian, James R., "Science and Public Policy," *Science,* **129,** 132 (1959).
2. Eidensheim, Julie, "Editor at Work," p. 193, New York, Farrar & Reinhart, Inc., 1939.
3. Sherrod, John, "The Library of Congress," *Science,* **127,** 959 (1958).
4. Shera, Jesse H., Kent, Allen, and Perry, James W., editors, "Information Systems in Documentation," p. 539, New York, Interscience Publishers, Inc., 1957.

"Any improbable event which would create maximum confusion if it did occur...will occur"

HERBERT McGURK

McGURKS LAW

At 8:45 the day seemed half over for Conrad who was asking a waiter to set four more places at the speakers' breakfast table. Invitations had been extended only to individuals presenting papers, but several non-speaking authors were imperturbably sipping orange juice.

The 9:30 press conference went smoothly except for one speaker who, contrary to conference rules, "plugged" his firm's products.

The ballroom was filled to capacity when the keynote session started at 10:30. Modulation of the public-address system gave each speaker a rich senatorial voice; warning lights at the lectern permitted session chairmen to maintain precise schedules; careful numbering kept projection slides in correct sequence; air-conditioning and upholstered seats contributed to general comfort. In fact, only one oversight marred an otherwise perfect meeting. There was no stair on which to mount the twenty-inch-high speakers' platform. This proved to be only a minor inconvenience until a strikingly attractive woman speaker, Grace McClellan, approached the platform in a tight skirt. However, she neither waited ceremoniously for stairs to appear, nor accepted the too-eager offers of a lift; she simply raised her skirt above her knees and climbed to the platform amid thunderous male applause.

Mr. Conrad was called from the session. The hotel was filled and could not accommodate two late registrants. Would Mr. Conrad help them? He led two wilted-looking gentlemen to the hotel sales manager who arranged that they occupy the first vacated rooms. They were lodged within the hour.

On the second day, the arrangements committee provided a service designed especially for the convenience of the conferrers. Airlines were invited to staff reconfirmation and ticketing booths outside the ballroom. Queues formed as soon as the booths opened, but Conrad was thoroughly puzzled and somewhat chagrined when the long lines suddenly evaporated. One enterprising conferrer had stepped from his thirty-man line into a telephone booth where he loudly reconfirmed his airline reservations in a matter of seconds. Despite this incident, the airlines, alerted to the conference's transportation needs, obligingly added extra flights.

The banquet started promptly, with hotel employees collecting tickets at the hall entrance. Conrad added an extra place-card to the head table. Besides the banquet speaker, session chairmen, and himself, he had a place set for Grace McClellan, the charming speaker who had earned the affection and respect of all those in the ballroom.

At the closing session, Mr. Conrad announced, ". . . again, thanks for your support and active participation. The hotel has extended the check-out time to 6:00 P.M. for those of you who wish to use recreational facilities this afternoon. To complete your list of conference attenders, a notice of late arrivals is being distributed. Following this session, there will be an open meeting of the evaluation committee. You are urged to come and suggest improvements for future conferences. . . ."

Evaluation of the Conference

Following Arthur Conrad's announcement, several conferrers attended the evaluation committee's open meeting. Walter Sumner presided. He spoke about committee goals and progress.

"The evaluation conference audits the extent to which conference objectives have been and are being achieved. It recommends follow-up action and suggests how future programs might be made more effective. It weighs the potential contribution of future conferences against probable man-power and expense. Appraisals and recommendations are based on information obtained through feedback techniques such as questionnaires, interviews, unsolicited advice, clipping bureaus, and open meetings like this."

The Questionnaire Technique. Questionnaires seem to be a fast and inexpensive technique for getting information. One man and a duplicating machine are all that are needed. Simple, direct answers, like yes, no, indifferent, fall into definite categories and can be readily tabulated. A questionnaire viewed through the eyes of a recipient, however, seems less like an ingenious probe and more like an unwelcome intruder. The recipient is likely to finger the pages and mutter, "What do they want this time? What do I get from this inquisition? What the devil does this third question mean? What are they prying for anyway? It's too long and complicated! CRUMPLE."

Despite the unfriendly receptions usually given to ill-conceived questionnaires, the evaluation committee enjoyed relative success with its written survey. Questions were worded to trigger honest, forthright, thoughtful replies. The first draft was pretested to improve clarity, objectivity, and content. As a result, ideas for new questions emerged. Opening questions were simplified to ensure continued interest. Questions were rearranged to stimulate the flow of replies. All ambiguous, biased, loaded, misleading, and empty questions were eliminated.

Pretesting brought to light ineffectual phrasing. For example, the committee wanted to know which promotional media were successful in reaching and influencing prospective conferrers. The preliminary questionnaire asked, "How did you learn of this conference?" Unfortunately, typical replies from the pretested sampling included, "from my boss," or "from an associate." Therefore, questions were reworded and retested, and a final one-page questionnaire printed as shown in Figure 7.1.

The following are some of the suggestions which Walter Sumner received in response to the questionnaire.

(1) Tell speakers to drive home their points faster. (If they don't strike oil in the first twenty minutes they should stop boring.)

(2) Station someone at the microphone amplifier to guard against high-pitched feedback whine.

(3) In old-time vaudeville, each group of performers was identified by an easel sign announcing its act. Similarly, if names were posted for every presentation, there might be greater rapport between speaker and audience, and a better climate for discussion.

(4) Keep the pace moving by minimizing the time allotted for introducing speakers. Supplement brief oral introductions with biographical notes printed in the program.

(5) Visual presentations might be better understood were two projectors used simultaneously. While one slide was giving an over-all view, a second could show component segments or partial views. Because both 35-mm and 3¼" x 4" slide projectors are

CONFERENCE QUESTIONNAIRE

By completing this form you will be helping us to make future conferences more profitable for you. Use the attached blank sheets for comments.

(1) To guide us in interpreting your reactions please give the name of your firm (company, college, etc.) _____
Product or services of your firm _____
Your department _____
Your position, or description of your work _____

(2) Have conference topics been fairly pertinent to your field of interest? Yes____ No____ Comments (Use blank sheets attached.)

(3) Was the general level of information exchange at formal sessions too elementary? Yes____ No____ Too theoretical? Yes____ No____ Just about right? Yes____ No____ Comments

(4) What topics would you like included in a future conference? _____
_____

(5) What benefits did you hope to derive from attending this conference?
_____

(6) In view of the benefits derived from this conference, do you recommend that we organize another conference? Yes____ No____ Comments

(7) To help us improve techniques of promotion, please list whatever conference publicity you or other persons in your firm received. _____
_____

(8) Did advance publicity give you an accurate preview of the conference? Yes____ No__ Comments

(9) Were you satisfied with the housing? Yes____ No____ The social? Yes____ No____ The banquet? Yes____ No____ The tour? Yes____ No____ Registration? Yes____ No____ Room arrangements? Yes____ No____ Comments

(10) Would you like commercial exhibits to be held in conjunction with a future conference? Yes____ No____ Comments

(11) Please write further criticisms, observations, or suggestions on the blank sheets attached. Thanks for you help.

Name (optional) _____

FIGURE 7.1

usually available, a second projection screen would be the only additional equipment required.

(6) Ask the dining room supervisor to increase his staff during the breakfast and luncheon rush.

(7) Seat the panel moderator at one end of the table so that he can see all panelists with a single glance.

Chairman Sumner assigned a subcommittee to analyze questionnaire replies thoroughly and to report its conclusions.

The Interview Technique. Walter Sumner described another technique used by the evaluation committee for gathering feedback information. Several committeemen were asked to be roving interviewers during the conference. Each man was selected for his ability to carry on informal conversation, sense true feelings, interpret technical commentary, and report objectively.

Interviewers spoke with a random sampling of conferrers during "free" periods. In only one respect did the sampling prove to be not very random. Ninety-six per cent of the conferrers were male, of whom six per cent were interviewed; four per cent were female, of whom 100 per cent were interviewed. An already-saddened committee statistician was heartily dismayed when he learned that one particularly lovely female registrant had been interviewed three times.

Despite this unrepresentative sampling, the interview technique had one obvious advantage. Feedback information could be obtained early enough to be useful during the conference. For example, the following problems were recorded by interviewers during the first conference day. Remedial action was initiated within hours after the interviewing was completed.

Problem. A topic of great interest to some conferrers was completely omitted from the program.

Solution. The evaluation committee decided to supplement regular afternoon seminars, designed to continue discussion of papers which had stirred audience response, with "sign-up" seminars, organized to provide forums for topics inadvertently omitted from the program. The following posters were prominently displayed: "Persons interested in participating in a seminar on _____ please sign below. If sufficient interest is shown, a time and place will be arranged."

Problem. Because session chairmen were not introduced, those whose backgrounds were not generally known had difficulty establishing rapport with the audience.

Solution. To improve communication between chairmen and audience, the evaluation committee decided that each chairman should be briefly introduced by the chairman of a preceding session.

Problem. Even where ample time was available, provocative talks sometimes ended with only a few perfunctory questions.

Solution. Since the chairman or moderator is responsible for maintaining lively discussion, he and a few pre-selected members of the audience should be prepared to revive faltering discussion by posing controversial questions. Speakers should be informed of "planted" questions beforehand so that they, too, can effectively lead conferrers toward fresh areas of inquiry.

Problem. Time was lost when speakers had to brief projection operators.

Solution. The evaluation committee decided that, to avoid these annoying huddles, a committeeman should sit with speakers and relay last-minute instructions to the projection operator before each talk.

Problem. Floor discussion was occasionally inaudible; too often session chairmen neglected to repeat statements into the platform microphone.

Solution. Walter Sumner's final reminder to session chairmen: "For heaven's sake, please repeat questions from the floor!"

Volunteered Feedback. Some unsolicited information will always find its way back to the evaluation committee. Unsolicited information can be categorized as "gripes" (justified and unjustified) and suggestions (reasonable and unreasonable). Such information is usually right to the point and often constructive.

Consider a campus-situated conference. The first group of registrants is housed in deluxe, wall-to-wall carpeted rooms at the university's ultra-modern hotel, Union Memorial Center. The last group occupies the student dormitory, Skidbarn Hall.

A distinguished, gray-haired conferrer enters Union Memorial Center to register.

The clerk says, "Sorry, Mr. Simms. We can only accommodate you in Skidbarn Hall."

"All right, I'd like a room with a bath, please."

"Sorry, Mr. Simms. Skidbarn has no private baths."

"All right, I'll double up."

"Skidbarn has no semi-private baths, either."

"Well, just how many people do share one bathroom, anyway?"

"Let me see, that would be everyone on the fourth floor. Forty, sir."

"FORTY! Who the hell do I look like? Joe College?"

And off stalks Mr. Simms to a downtown hotel, righteously indignant. A man of his age and status is not disposed to climb four flights of stairs carrying luggage to double-bunk in a room without air-conditioning, or to surrender the comfort of a private bath for the bustle of a community "john." Though he was not asked about it, Mr. Simms made known his inconvenience; as a result, the evaluation committee recommended that in the future more consideration be given to housing senior conferrers.

Unsolicited information is not always constructive, however, and frequently can be disregarded. Consider conferrer Thornton in the midst of liplashing a quivering girl at the registration desk.

"Are you trying to tell me that you refuse to return my banquet money, Miss?"

"It's nothing personal, Mr. Thornton, but no refunds can be made on the day of the banquet. The committee has to guarantee your meal whether or not you actually dine here."

"Come, come girl! Surely you don't expect me to stand idly by while my banquet money is being brazenly robbed. Take me to the director!"

"Oh, Mr. Banquet Chairman! Mr. Thornton wants to speak with you."

"Now look here, Mr. Chairman. A salesman has just invited me to dinner and I demand my banquet ticket refund. I will not be victimized by your money-grabbing organization."

"Mr. Thornton, our banquet guarantee obligations have been carefully described to you. This conference is sponsored by a nonprofit organization. We accepted your reservation in good faith. . . ."

"Who's the head of your organization? Take me to the top!"

The Clipping Bureau. Feedback information regarding press reaction to the conference as well as the extent of news coverage can be obtained from a clipping bureau. Scissors in hand, clipping-service agencies will scan both the general press and the technical press; they will clip any articles or references which name a specific conference or organization. There is usually a fixed fee plus additional charges for each clipping. Several nation-wide bureaus are listed in *Writer's Market,* published by Writer's Digest, Cincinnati 10, Ohio.

When a clipping service is retained for publicity, the public relations committee should assemble a promotion scrapbook with clippings pasted next to related news release copy so that future committees can pattern their releases after the more successful prototypes.

The Open Evaluation Committee Meeting. The open meeting is a most effective way to assess conference reaction. Walter Sumner held his evaluation committee meeting after the last conference session; he worked from the following list of questions.

AGENDA

(1) What feedback information obtained from conference questionnaires and interviews will help evaluate the effectiveness of the conference? Can any pertinent information be added?

(2) Were the "right" people attracted to the conference? Did conferrers engage in worthwhile give-and-take participation?

(3) Did advance publicity give an accurate picture of conference objectives?

(4) Were advance registrants able to prepare themselves adequately for conference participation?

(5) Were conference objectives met? Were conferrers satisfied?

(6) What improvements for future conference planning are possible?

(7) What recommendations can be proposed for future conferences? When should another conference be held, if at all?

Ideas generated at the open committee meeting in response to these questions were reported to the general conference chairman.

Follow-up Action

The final report of the evaluation committee was presented in three sections: (1) conferrer suggestions; (2) committee suggestions for clean-up and follow-up action; (3) committee suggestions for improving future conferences.

Conferrer Suggestions. Conferrer feedback information was reported for consideration by future committees. Conferrer reaction ranged from such general comments as, "program was too theoretical," to such specific observations as, "breakfast coffee was terrible." The gamut of commentary also included advice: "Screen out monotone speakers; differentiate M.D.'s from Ph.D.'s in printed program; reduce the use of flashbulbs during talks; distribute more ashtrays; eliminate fashion show from ladies' program—too expensive; rent more comfortable tour buses; aim more promotion at educators, military personnel, consultants, and international leaders; schedule more speakers at each session; schedule fewer speakers at each session; insist that outrageous prices at hotel bars be reduced; encourage more informal attire. . . ."

Clean-up and Follow-up. After conferrers assemble, deliberate, and disband, the conference organization still must perform several functions. The following check list of clean-up activities was included in the final report: "Thank all committeemen and speakers; mail refunds to advance registrants unable to attend; distribute a 'conference roundup' news release; promote membership in the conference sponsoring organization; distribute a final statement of finances to all committee chairmen; compile committee reports, form letters, minutes, and mailing lists in a conference binder; complete and distribute printed transactions. . . ."

After a group has been painstakingly assembled at a technical conference, what follow-up action will ensure continued communication? Perhaps a periodic newsletter should be printed and regional seminars organized. After a new concept has been accepted by conferrers, what follow-up action will promote general acceptance? Perhaps a special monograph should be published. Conflicting terminology inhibits conference discussion. What follow-up will eliminate confusion and inefficiency? A standards committee might be established.

The most effective follow-up for any independent conference group may be affiliation with a progressive association or society. Existing organizations offer a proven, ready-made vehicle for distributing newsletters, organizing regional meetings, publishing monographs, and establishing standards.

Improving Future Conferences. The final evaluation report did not attempt to rehash mechanical details. Individual committee reports proposed improvements regarding specific operational problems. The evaluation committee sought basic areas in need of improvement and found three: pretesting, the conferrer, and secret information.

Pretesting. Before major commitments are made, it might be prudent to pretest the proposed conference on a reduced scale. A local, one-day, informal, pilot conference might help answer the following questions. Will a full-blown conference be fruitful? Who should attend? What should be discussed? The decision to pretest, however, must be carefully weighed before each proposed conference.

The Conferrer. The evaluation report emphasized a paradox: although only five per cent of the conferrers were speakers, they received ninety-five per cent of the pre-conference information. More attention to non-speakers would pay dividends. The evaluation committee suggested that an informative advance newsletter—including short articles on conferrer etiquette; what to pack; briefing colleagues not able to attend; note-taking; being a conferrer, not a contestant; the art of good listening—be distributed to all conferrers. The evaluation report cited the following example on "listening" to illustrate how the newsletter might guide conferrers toward more constructive participation.

"If you were one of several children you may recall that your brothers and sisters who spoke the loudest got the most parental attention. At school, if you raised your hand frequently to speak, your grades were probably good. In our competitive society, you advance by getting your views across. At conferences, however, you gain the most by listening. As Oliver Wendell Holmes said, 'It is the province of knowledge to speak and it is the privilege of wisdom to listen.'

"To listen well does not mean to listen supinely; it means to make an honest effort to understand the views being expressed. To listen well does not mean to assume, 'oh, it's just another variation of an old theme'; it means to get all the facts before making generalizations."

Secret Information. The withholding of pertinent information, either by industrial firms or governmental agencies, reduces the value of technical conferences. The evaluation committee report urged the conference organization to announce, vehemently, opposition to excessive, thoughtless, or unnecessary censorship of scientific information. The committee was in complete accord with the following statement by Norbert Wiener in his book, The Human Use of Human Beings. "Information is more a matter of process than of storage . . . No amount of scientific research, carefully recorded in books and papers, and then put into libraries with labels of secrecy, will be adequate to protect us for any length of time in a world where the effective level of information is perpetually advancing." [1]

Reference

1. Weiner, Norbert, "The Human Use of Human Beings," pp. 121-122, New York, Doubleday & Co., Inc., 1954.

CONFERENCE · TABLE · CONFERENCE · TABLE · CONFERENCE

CONFERENCES

THE · IDEAL · PATTERN · FOR · COMMITTEE · CONFERENCES :

COMMUNICATION
CONVENE ON TIME
ASK FOR COMMENTS
TO THE PROPOSED
AGENDA · · · OPEN
WITH A STATEMENT
OF OBJECTIVES · ·
NEGLECT NO ONE
SPARK FULL CON-
STRUCTIVE PARTIC
IPATION · · · FOCUS
ATTENTION ON CON
FLICTING OPINIONS
· · EXAMINE FACTS
BEFORE LEAPING TO
SOLUTIONS · · · RE-
CORD HIGHLIGHTS
OF CONFERENCE
DELIBERATIONS · ·
· ENCOURAGE PEN-
ETRATING EVAL-
UATION WITH PROB
ING QUESTIONS · · NAIL
DECISIONS WHICH GAIN
GROUP SUPPORT · · CONCLUDE
WITH ASSIGNMENTS FOR FOLLOW
UP ACTION OR FOR ADDITIONAL
FACT-FINDING · · · END ON TIME
PROPOSE A DATE FOR THE NEXT
MEETING · · ·   SEND EACH
CONFEREE MIN-   UTES SUMMARIZ-
ING CONCLUSIONS   AND ASSIGNMENTS

8 *The Committee Conference*

Technical conferences are often organized by means of a series of committee conferences—smaller gatherings intended to resolve problems through discussion (more-or-less democratic).

Some individuals prefer to resolve problems alone. They claim that group deliberation is inferior to personal deliberation. Dr. Alan T. Waterman, National Science Foundation Director, said, ". . . the tendency of the group is to be conservative. . . ." [1] Howard Roark, protagonist in Ayn Rand's "The Fountainhead," asserts more strongly, "There is no such thing as a collective thought. An agreement reached by a group of men is only a compromise or an average drawn upon many individual thoughts." [2] Even men explaining conference techniques have written, "Honest, reasonable compromise is the essence of good conference work. . . ." [3] "There is give and take and compromise in a democratic discussion." [4]

Without doubt a group can dilute potent ideas, dull keen insights, scar sensible proposals, and compromise flawless plans into oblivion; but *individual creativity need not be submerged in group conformity.* Productive, resourceful, efficient problem-solving conferences are possible.

Few situations offer greater opportunity for constructive problem-solving than does the committee conference within a volunteer organization. Conferrers are hand-picked from among the

119

most able candidates in the community, the nation, and the world. Discussion is rarely inhibited by the presence of company superiors. Most important, participation is based not on a memo-mandate from the front office but on personal dedication to the task at hand.

Whether the committee conference compromises by taking the "happy" middle-road or rises to find the truly best solution depends on several factors. Have the most apt problems been chosen for group consideration? Have a capable chairman and team been selected? Will each committeeman have the opportunity to exercise his own problem-solving ingenuity before every conference? Can the chairman create an atmosphere in which each individual will be inspired to volunteer his best efforts?

Problems

What types of problems should committees tackle? The problem must be important, not only to the organization but to every committee member. Whether the banquet dessert should be petits fours or meringue glacé is not really a problem worthy of group resolution.

A committee should consider a problem only after all germane information is available. How many conference hours have melted away in torrid debate for want of a few facts!

A committee should consider a problem only if it is complex enough to provide a group challenge. For example, selecting a program for a technical conference will challenge the competence of any group. In fact, one person rarely, if ever, would be capable of programing a comprehensive technical conference within a reasonable length of time. Can you imagine anyone knowledgeable enough to plan a program even on so narrow a topic as, say, "nuclear instrumentation"? Such a program might cover radiation measurement for medical therapy, aircraft propulsion, food preservation, genetic studies, rubber vulcanization, airborne contamination, botanical research, space exploration, and reactor safety. Clearly, a group can better embrace and resolve the problem of arranging a technical program than can an individual.

Chairman

The chairman of a committee conference must be versatile. He should be able to think ahead with precision; phrase his thoughts clearly; react constructively to the unexpected; analyze personalities with sensitivity and acumen. He should have vitality, a sense of humor, tact, diplomacy, and an even temperament.

The chairman's resourcefulness is continually challenged by the conferrer's desire for self-recognition. Against his natural instinct, the conferrer is expected to throw his best ideas into the melting pot and watch them as they are stirred into anonymity. What does the conferrer gain? The chairman must conduct a meeting which will allow conferrers to sharpen their wits, and to feel that they are playing an essential role in establishing important decisions as well as gaining the approbation of respected colleagues.

Too often, committee chairmen are appointed solely because they are well known or well liked. A candidate for conference leader must be able to elicit sound group decisions by directing inquiry, defining terms, testing solutions, resolving conflict, injecting enthusiasm, smoothing emotions, and synthesizing conclusions.

No book can create a leader; but if men with leadership potential can be made to appreciate conference responsibilities and learn the ground rules, their meetings will be more effective.

Conferrers

In choosing committee members, the chairman must anticipate likely problems in order to match the capabilities of the committee with the demands of the situation. A chairman should be as critical of potential committeemen as an attorney is of prospective jurymen. Each committeeman should have enough initiative to analyze the problems from his own viewpoint, tenacity not to compromise without good reason, discernment to perceive how other ideas might improve his own, and confidence to accept the best decisions regardless of personality involvements.

How many persons constitute the "right" number for an effective conference committee meeting? The following table presents the divergent opinions of several authorities.

Conferrers should number at least:	The ideal number of conferrers is:	Conferrers should number no more than:	Reference
6	7	9	5
5-6	9	12-13	6
8-10	12-14	16	7
8	12-15	20	8
10	16	45	9

Professor C. Northcote Parkinson describes the ideal deliberative body in a refreshing style. "We should eventually be able ... to learn the formula by which the optimum number of committee members may be determined. Somewhere between the number 3 (where a quorum is impossible to collect) and approximately 21 (when the whole organism begins to perish), there lies a golden number." [10]

The "golden" number, averaged from the five ideal numbers in the preceding table, is 11.7. (And the author prefers even fewer conferrers in a decision-making group.)

Preliminaries

Agenda. Never call a committee meeting without first distributing an agenda. Keep it brief but include meeting date and place, names and affiliations of committee members, starting time, planned duration, delineation of problems, and a statement of meeting goals. Append supporting data, tabulations, budgets, charts.

Problem-resolution Plan. Careful planning is required of the conference leader and may take the following form:

conferences, or where calls must come through, a remote message-writer (which lights up when a message is being transmitted) might be convenient. Someone nearby need simply tear off the written message and deliver it.

(3) Will visual and auditory aids be delivered in time to have them checked and have replacements made, if necessary? Are spare parts, like projector bulbs, available?

(4) Does the meeting room have dark shades, electrical outlets, and spotlights, if needed?

(5) If all committeemen do not know each other, have name cards been prepared?

(6) Have chalkboards, flip pads, chalk, erasers, crayons, felt ink markers, easels, pointers, thumbtacks, water, glasses, ash trays, and coat racks been provided?

Conducting the Meeting

The success of a meeting depends largely on its leader. Conferrers provide a motivating power which the leader must steer. Should committee conferences be democratic? Pure discussion is the essence of democracy, yet decisions are reached more slowly (and not necessarily any better) than if discussion is directed by a somewhat autocratic hand. Democracy is based on the theory of equal opportunity. The conference leader can give all conferrers an equal opportunity to express their ideas; he cannot give them equal time. He must assume responsibility for stifling unimaginative, cantankerous, or irrelevant remarks.

The technique of control lies in proficient questioning. Questions can introduce topics, provoke ideas, encourage participation, and modulate discussion. Conference questions have been categorized as "overhead," "direct," "reverse," and "relay." [11]

Overhead questions are addressed to all conferrers and are particularly useful in starting and ending discussion. For example, the overhead question, "Does the group believe that exhibits should be arranged in conjunction with the technical conference?" starts discussion; the question, "Does anyone have pertinent comments to add before we summarize?" wraps up discussion.

Direct questions are asked of specific individuals to encourage participation, develop a topic, elicit facts, rouse an inattentive conferrer, prick an expansive soliloquy, or direct a meandering discourse.

Reverse and relay questions help the chairman maintain his impartiality. Suppose conferrer Fensitter asks, "In your opinion, Mr. Chairman, should we sponsor exhibits?" He can avoid taking sides by asking a reverse question: "How do you view the merits of sponsoring exhibits, Mr. Fensitter?" Or, he can broaden the discussion with a relay question: "Would Messrs. Brown, Jones, and Johnson offer their views on this complex problem?"

Despite such profuse questioning, conference chairmen are not quiz masters. They do not interrogate to check a conferrer's knowledge, but rather to encourage and direct his participation.

Visual and auditory aids, a problem-resolution plan, good meeting facilities, and thoughtful questioning all contribute to the success of a committee conference. Obstacles do exist, however, and may trap a chairman and prevent his meeting from getting anywhere. A path circumventing these obstacles might be mapped in advance were it not for that major obstruction, present at every conference—that unpredictable element—people.

Some people who hinder progress are talkative; others are tight-lipped. Some are aggressive, others retiring; some are inscrutable, others transparent. Most appear reasonable—until they reach the conference table. Then, as the agenda is unfurled, a subtle metamorphosis transforms everyday people into "obstructionists."

There are no pat rules to guide the chairman. With his wits alone he must make allies out of adversaries. He can arm himself by knowing his enemy—by being on the lookout for: the purist, who is interested more in splitting hairs then in solving problems; the oversensitive egotist, who classifies all persons challenging his views as malicious vendettists; the dodger, who won't take a firm stand on any issue except sex and sin; the silent auditor, who takes in everything and contributes nothing; the stubborn reactionary, who opposes everything except "the way we did it the last time"; the relentless orator, who prefers talking to thinking; the infallible expert, who makes snap judgments about every question and defends his position to the end; the persistent plodder, who keeps reintroducing the same idea (in different words) after each rejection.

Let the following acrostic be your guide to conducting better meetings.

C onvene on time. Ask for comments on the proposed agenda.
O pen with a statement of objectives.
N eglect no one. Encourage full, constructive participation.
F ocus attention on conflicting opinions.
E xamine facts before leaping to conclusions.
R ecord highlights of conference deliberations.
E ncourage thoughtful evaluation. Ask probing questions.
N ail decisions supported by the group.
C onclude with assignments for follow-up action.
E nd on time. Propose a date for the next meeting.
S end minutes summarizing conclusions and assignments to each conferrer.

References

1. Waterman, Alan T., *Saturday Review*, p. 52 (June 6, 1959).
2. Rand, Ayn, "The Fountainhead," p. 700, New York, American Library of World Literature, Inc., 1952.
3. Loney, Glen M., "Briefing and Conference Techniques," p. 186, New York, McGraw-Hill Book Company, Inc., 1959.
4. Stigers, M. F., "Making Conference Programs Work," p. 120, New York, McGraw-Hill Book Company, Inc., 1944.
5. Zelko, Harold P., "Successful Conference and Discussion Techniques," p. 144, New York, McGraw-Hill Book Company, Inc., 1957.
6. Strauss, Bert and Frances, "New Ways to Better Meetings," p. 128, New York, The Viking Press, 1955.
7. Stigers, M. F., "Making Conference Programs Work," p. 11, New York, McGraw-Hill Book Company, Inc., 1944.
8. Maclin, E. S., and McHenry, P. T., "Conference Leader Training," p. 70, National Foreman's Institute, 1945.
9. Cooper, Alfred M., "How to Conduct Conferences," p. 185, New York, McGraw-Hill Book Company, Inc., 1942.
10. Parkinson, C. Northcote, "Parkinson's Law," p. 44, Boston, Houghton Mifflin Company, 1957.
11. "Conference Leadership," AF Manual 50.8, p. 42, Department of the Air Force, 1953.

Appendix I

TYPICAL EXHIBIT CONTRACT

APPLICATION FOR SPACE
AMERICAN SCIENCE SOCIETY EXHIBIT

Municipal Auditorium, Showville, December 27-29

Date of Application _____

Application for exhibit space at rentals shown on the floor plan and in compliance with the exhibit regulations contained in this contract.

Preferred booth number(s):

1st choice _____ 2nd choice _____ 3rd choice _____ 4th choice _____
State briefly what your exhibit will include: (Please use generic terms rather than trade names.) _____

_____

Space rental includes: general illumination; once-a-day janitorial service; watchmen services for off-hours; removal, storage, and return of empty shipping crates; an exhibit listing in the official program; registration badges for booth personnel; and, if desired, a uniform 8-ft high draped background with a two-line sign and 4-ft high draped side dividers. Space rental does not include: air, water, drainage, gas, electricity, private telephones, booth furnishings, insurance, uncrating, crating, and shipping costs.

In order that appropriate space be allocated, please check which services your exhibit will require: air____ water____ drainage____ gas____ 220 volt a-c electricity____. Will you use a mobile or trailer display? _____.

Please enclose check for 25 per cent of booth rental, made payable to American Science Society (111 Home Avenue, Hometown), the remainder to be sent within 30 days after this application has been accepted and booth space assigned.

Name of organization _____

Address _____

Individual's name _____Position _____
Signature _____Telephone _____
Your application for exhibit space will be promptly confirmed.

EXHIBIT REGULATIONS INDEX

REGULATIONS

1. *Exhibit Dates and Hours*

Tuesday, December 27—12:00 P.M. to 10:00 P.M.
Wednesday, December 28—12:00 P.M. to 6:00 P.M.
Thursday, December 29—12:00 P.M. to 4:00 P.M.
(Note: Morning hours are reserved for conference sessions. The Society's banquet is held Wednesday evening. Since general interest tends to wane, the exhibit closes early on the final day.)

2. *Installation of Exhibits*

Exhibits may be installed starting at 8:00 A.M., Monday, December 26. Installation must be completed by 10:00 A.M. Tuesday, December 27, so that aisles may be swept for the noon opening. Installation is prohibited during open exhibition hours.

3. *Removal of Exhibits*

All exhibits must remain intact until the final closing, Thursday, December 29, at 4:00 P.M. All exhibits must be removed from Municipal Auditorium by 5:00 P.M. Friday, December 30th.

4. *Character of Exhibits*

All exhibits must be related to the interests served by the American Science Society. The exhibit manager reserves the right to prohibit undignified exhibits. Contests, prize drawings, noisemakers, "cheese cake" displays, and side show tactics are prohibited. The noise level of an exhibit must neither detract from nor interfere with other exhibits. Booths shall not be used for employment solicitation.

5. *Subletting Space*

No exhibitor shall sublet, assign, or apportion the space allotted to him without the consent of the exhibit manager.

6. *Safety*

All decorative materials must be fireproof and must comply with appropriate safety codes. All operating equipment must have safety devices.

7. *Damage*

Exhibitors are liable for any damage caused by fastening display fixtures to the auditorium building. Exhibitors must provide drip pans for machinery requiring lubrication.

8. *Maximum Display Height*

The maximum display height is indicated on the exhibit floor plan.

9. *Available Utilities*

Electrical service includes 110 and 220 volt single phase 60 cycle alternating current; 220 volt three phase alternating current; 115 and 230 volt direct current. Special lighting and power connections can be supplied. Over-current protection must be provided.
Gas, water, drainage, and compressed air are available. Supply pressures, connection sizes, and gas analysis will be furnished upon request.
Contract all required utilities and installation labor directly with the Municipal Auditorium management.

10. *Available Services*

The following may be arranged through the exhibit manager: booth furnishings, carpeting, special decorations, sign-painting, private telephone service, photographic service, and floral service. Common labor, carpenters, painters, private guards, and special cleaning services may be arranged directly with the Municipal Auditorium management. Exhibitors are encouraged to consign their shipping and drayage needs to the official contractor, S. W. James, 100 Showville Avenue, Showville.

11. *Shipping Instructions*

All incoming shipments must be prepaid. Address parcel post and railway express shipments as follows: exhibitor's name, booth number, American Science Society Exhibit, Municipal Auditorium, Showville. Address railroad and motor freight shipments as follows: exhibitor's name, booth number,

American Science Society Exhibit, Municipal Auditorium, c/o S. W. James, 100 Showville Avenue, Showville. Mail S. W. James a copy of your bill of lading.

12. *Exhibit Registration Badges*

General admission to the exhibit will be by badge only. Badges for booth attendants will be provided in advance on request.

13. *Cancellation*

Cancellation of this contract by the exhibitor prior to March 1 of the exhibit year subjects him to forfeiture of deposit; cancellation after that date subjects him to forfeiture of total amount paid.

Appendix II

CONFERENCE SUCCESS RATING FORM

(only for the mathematically inclined conferrer)

Conferences may be numerically rated on how well they satisfy conferrer needs. Rating conferences is not merely an academic exercise. It forces organizers to consider all elements necessary for conference success and to appreciate their interdependence.

Conference success depends on the following elements: worthwhile information, effective presentation, audience feedback, and an appropriate environment. The relationship of these four elements is expressed in equation (1).

$$CSR = IR \times PR \times FR \times ER \qquad (1)$$

where CSR = conference success rating
IR = information rating
PR = presentation rating
FR = feedback rating
ER = environment rating

Certain factors are crucial for conference success. For example, if no audience feedback is generated, conference communication is impaired, despite basically good information. (Without feedback, the information could be read at home faster, more selectively, more comfortably, and at less expense.) If the information is simply a rehash of previous reports, conferrers cannot benefit despite how dramatic the presentation may be. Throughout the following equations, each factor is numerically weighted in proportion to its contribution to over-all conference success.

One other consideration is required to establish the rating equations—conference objectives. In writing the IR (information rating) equation, provision must be made to reflect the type of information which conference planners intended for the meeting. In other words, if the explicit intent was to present new information in only 30 per cent of the conference papers, no penalty should be assigned to the remaining 70 per cent of the information because it is of the survey type. K_1 and K_2 are included in Equation (2) to reflect the intended makeup of conference information.

$$IR = (K_1R_1 + K_2R_2)(R_3)(R_4)(.8R_5 + .2)(.7R_6 + .3) \qquad (2)$$

where IR = information rating

K_1 = that portion of conference information intended to reflect new developments and new interpretations

133

$K_2 =$ that portion of conference information intended to review or survey the field under consideration

$K_1 + K_2 = 1$

$$R_1 = \left(\frac{\text{new information}}{\text{redundant information}} \right)$$

$$R_2 = \left(\frac{\text{comprehensive information}}{\text{spotty information}} \right)$$

$$R_3 = \left(\frac{\text{pertinent information}}{\text{unrelated information}} \right)$$

$$R_4 = \left(\frac{\text{authoritative information}}{\text{unreliable information}} \right)$$

$$R_5 = \left(\frac{\text{provocative information}}{\text{pedestrian information}} \right)$$

$$R_6 = \left(\frac{\text{penetrating depth, useful scope}}{\text{superficial depth, excessive scope}} \right)$$

$$PR = (.7R_7 + .3)(.7R_8 + .3)(.5R_9 + .5)(.4R_{10} + .6) \qquad (3)$$

where PR = presentation rating

$$R_7 = \left(\frac{\text{stimulating presentation}}{\text{dull presentation}} \right)$$

$$R_8 = \left(\frac{\text{clear presentation}}{\text{confusing presentation}} \right)$$

$$R_9 = \left(\frac{\text{concise presentation}}{\text{prolix presentation}} \right)$$

$$R_{10} = \left(\frac{\text{well-organized presentation}}{\text{rambling presentation}} \right)$$

$$FR = (.9R_{11} + .1)(.7R_{12} + .3)(.5R_{13} + .5)(K_1R_{14} + K_2) \qquad (4)$$

where FR = feedback rating

$$R_{11} = \left(\frac{\text{compatibility of information and audience}}{\text{information—audience mismatched}} \right)$$

$$R_{12} = \left(\frac{\text{directed audience feedback}}{\text{weak chairmanship}} \right)$$

$$R_{13} = \left(\frac{\text{effective audience size}}{\text{audience size inadequate or unwieldy}} \right)$$

$$R_{14} = \left(\frac{\text{audience pre-orientation}}{\text{no audience preparation}} \right)$$

K_1 and K_2: see equation (2)

Index